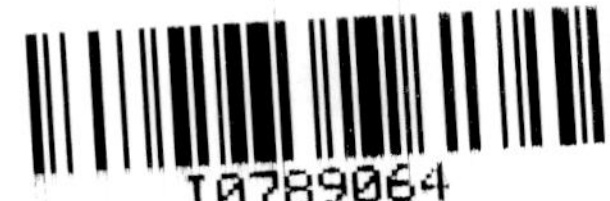

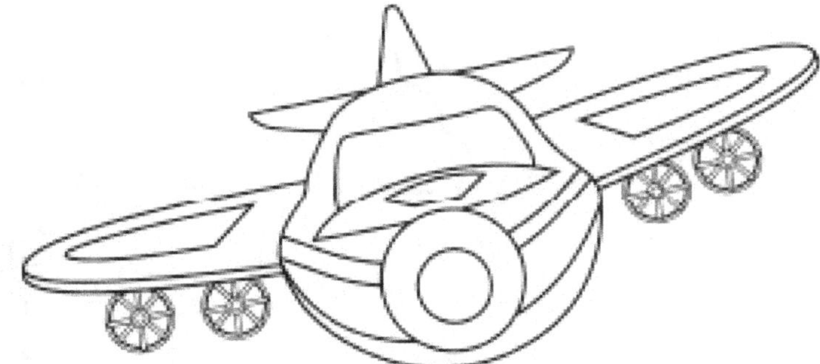

Trucks
Planes
and Cars

Coloring Books

by taha coloring

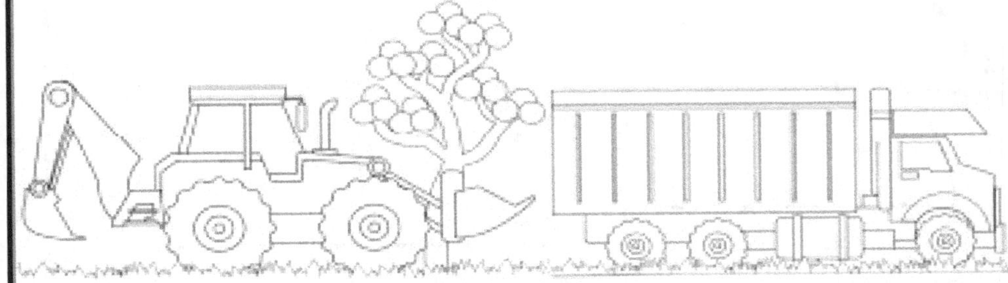

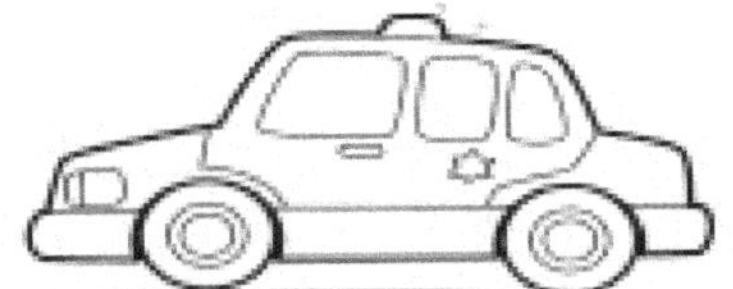

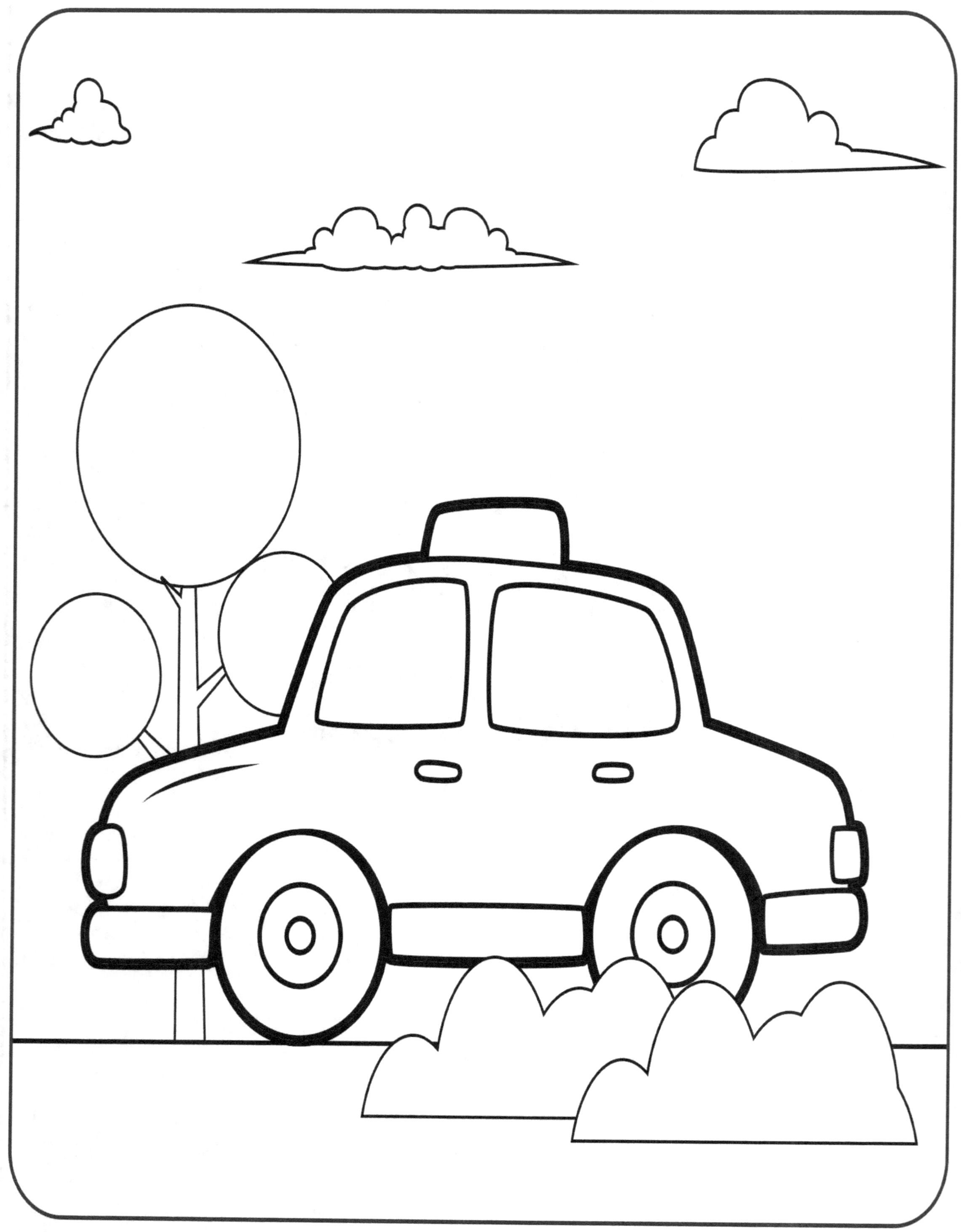

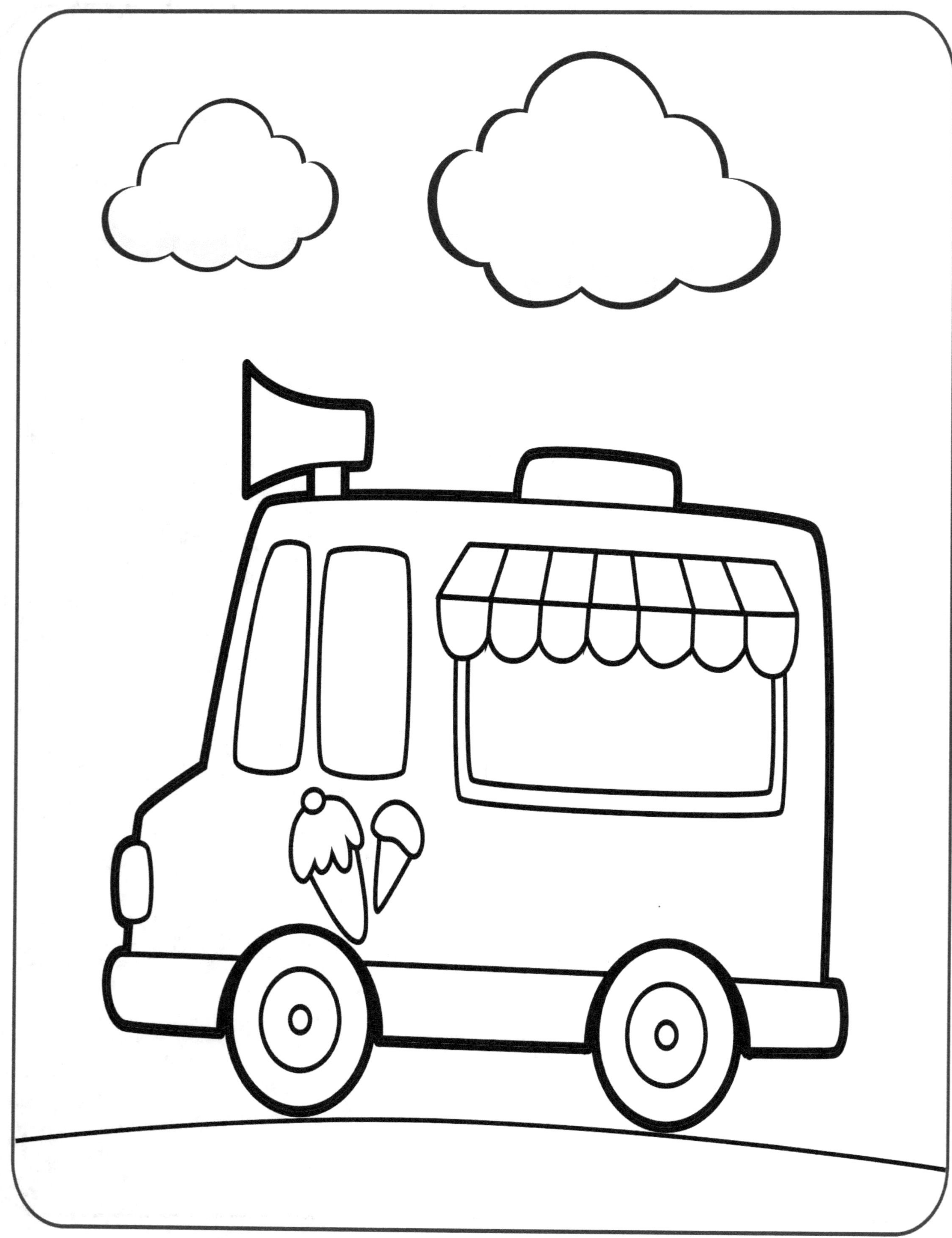

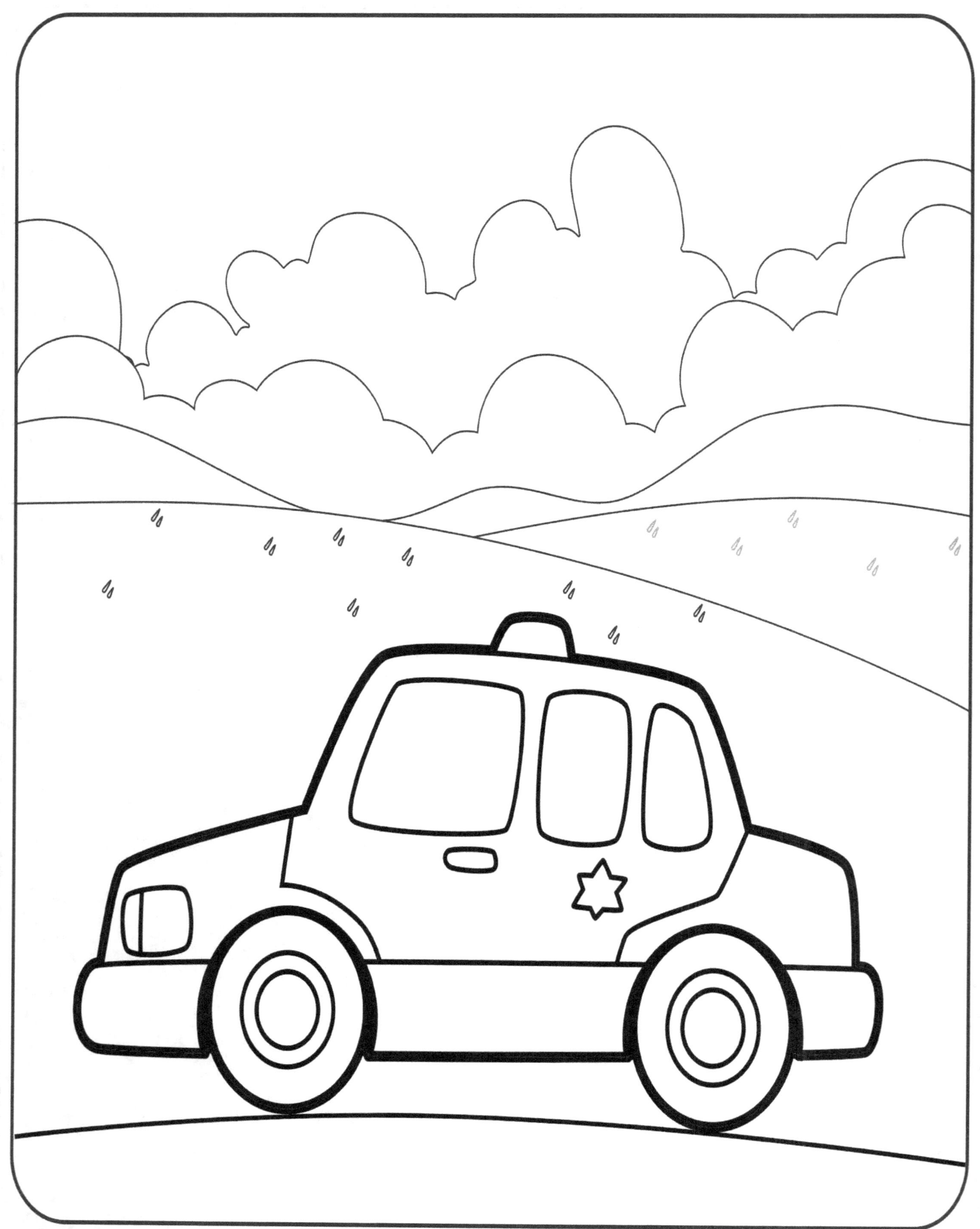

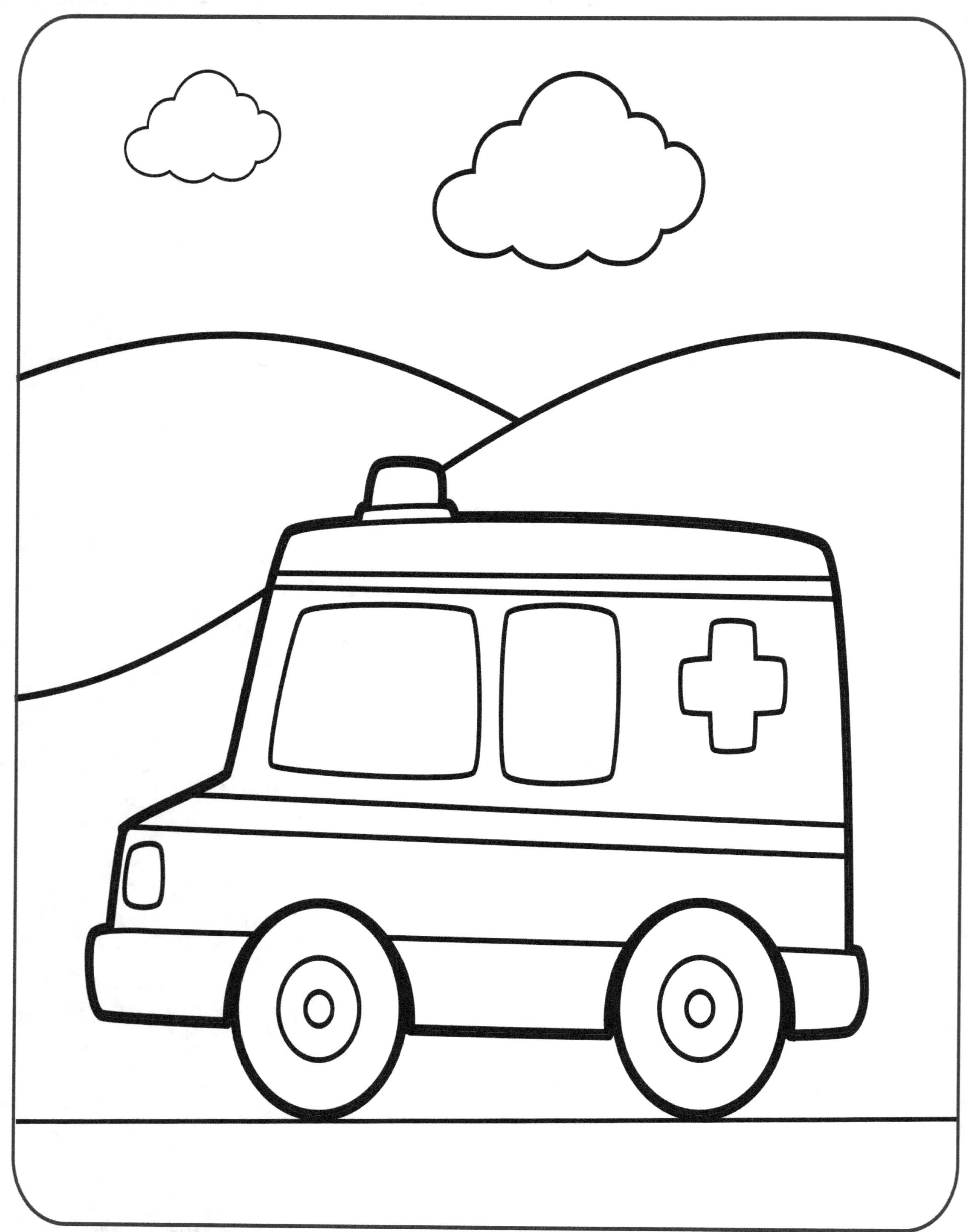

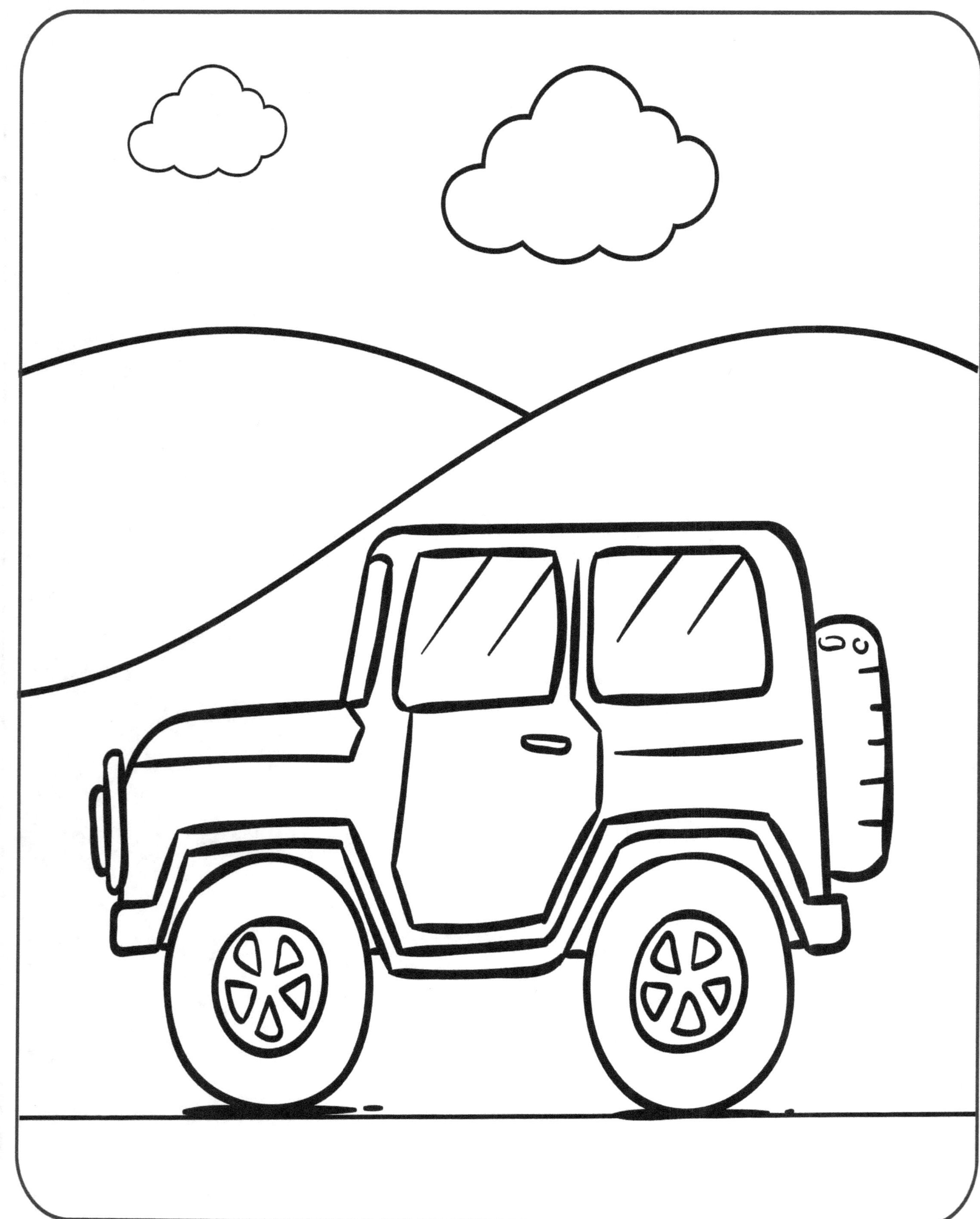

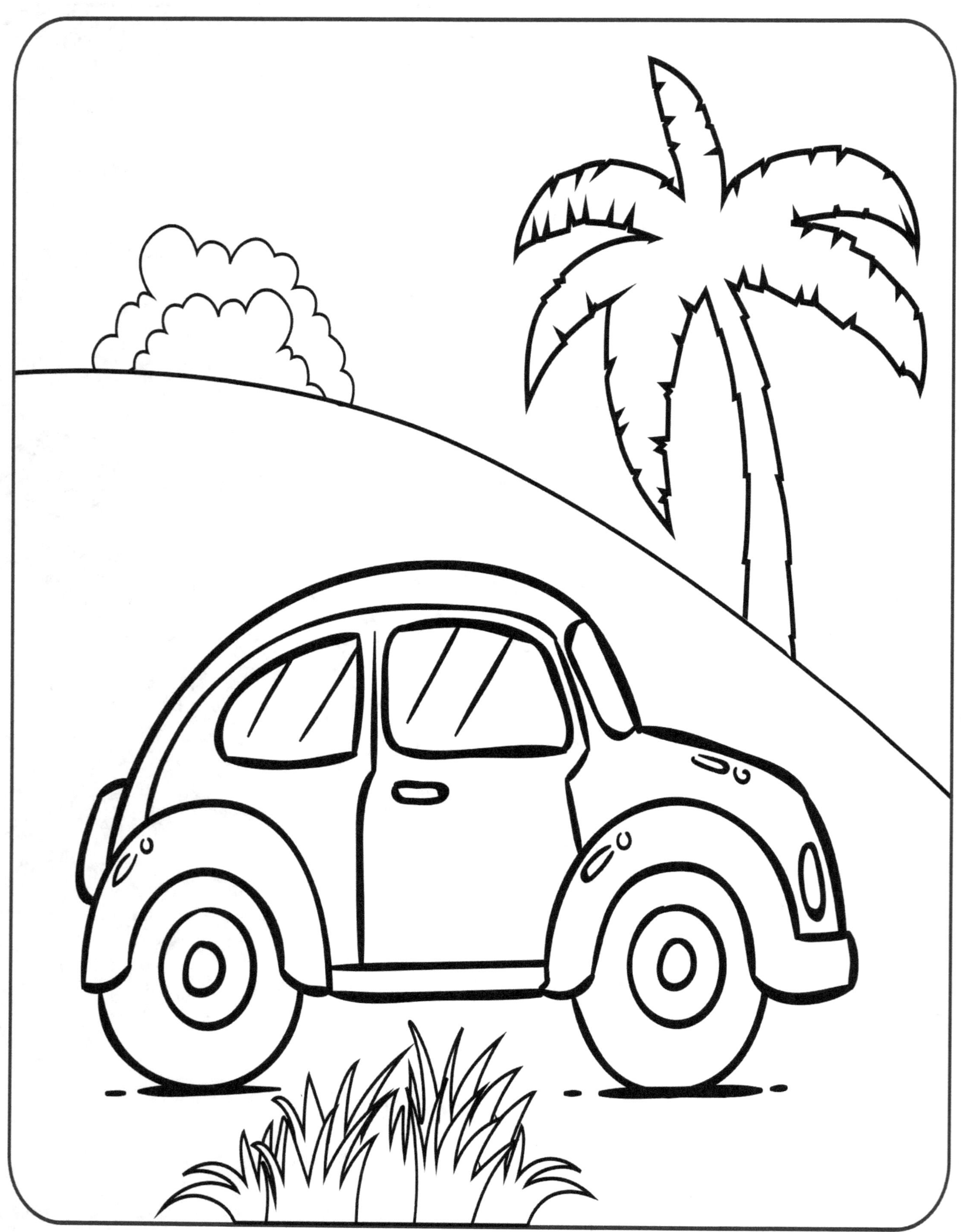

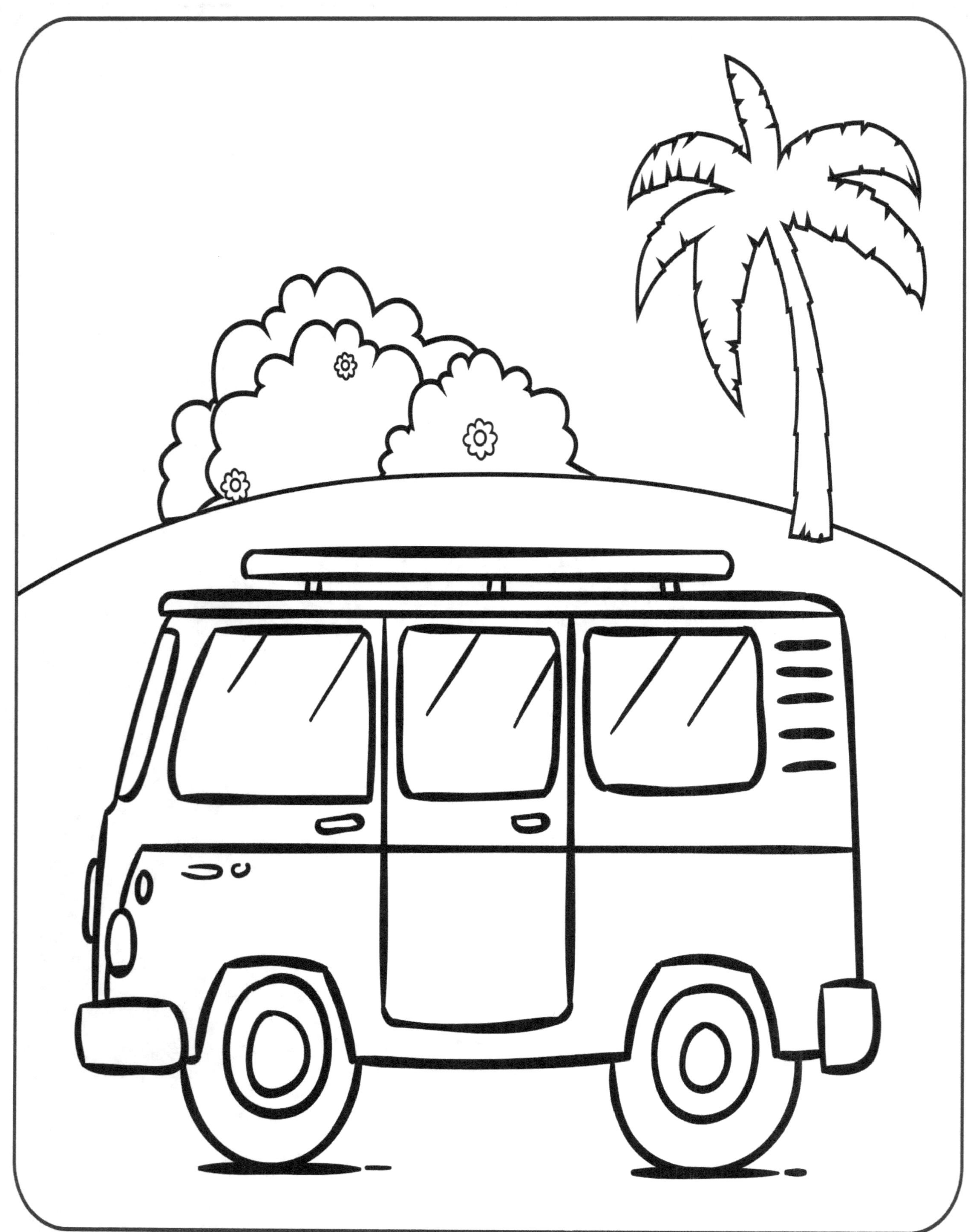

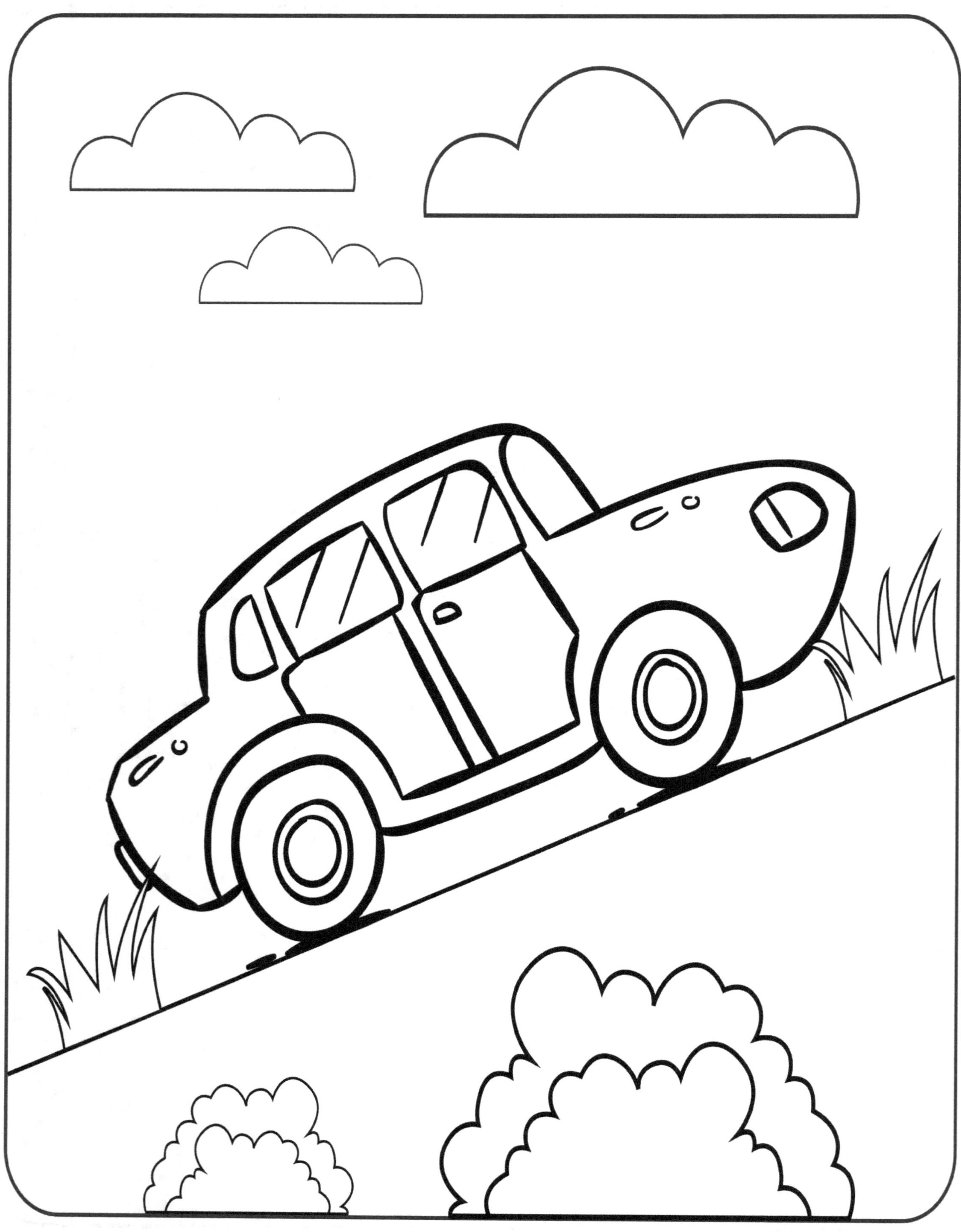

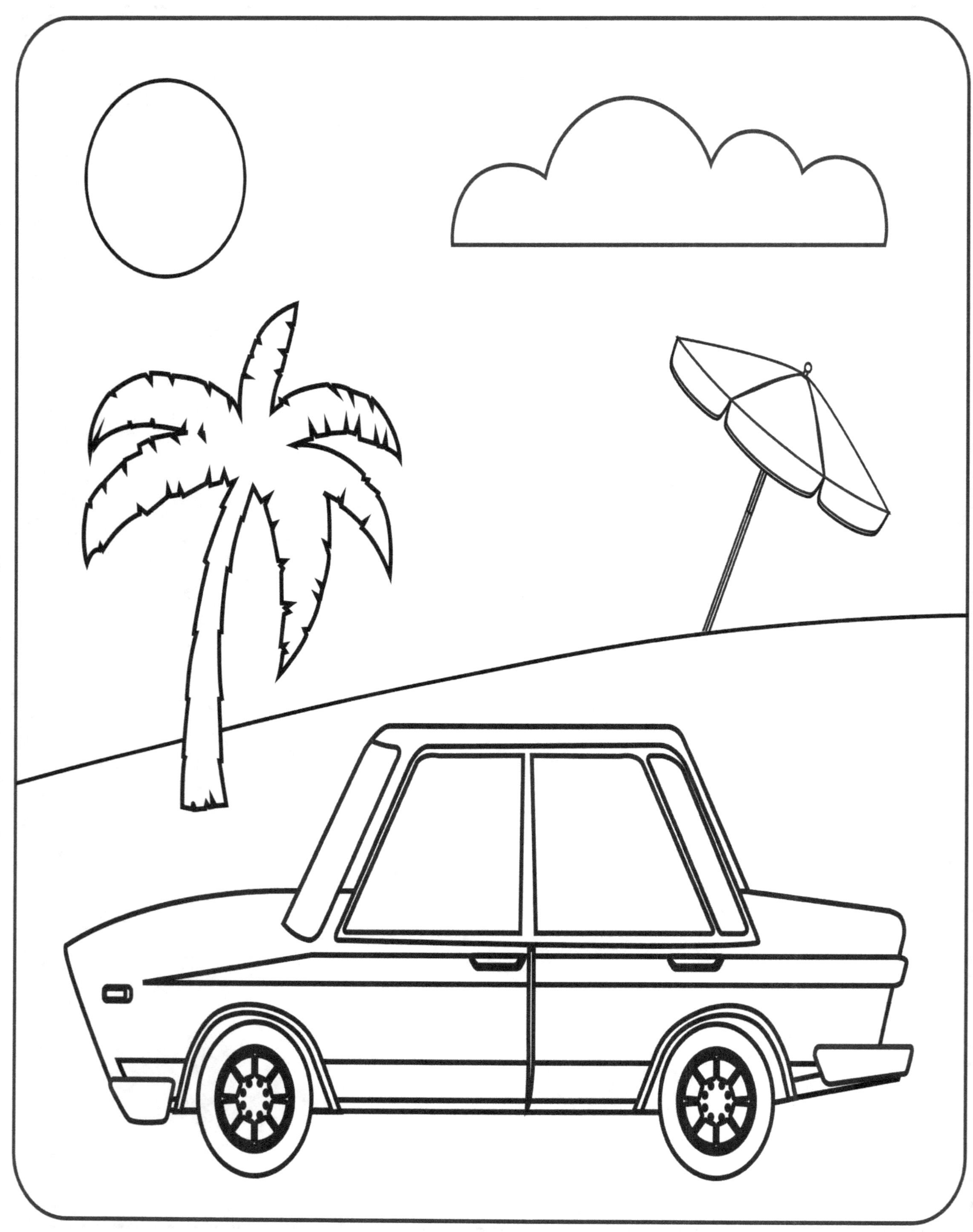

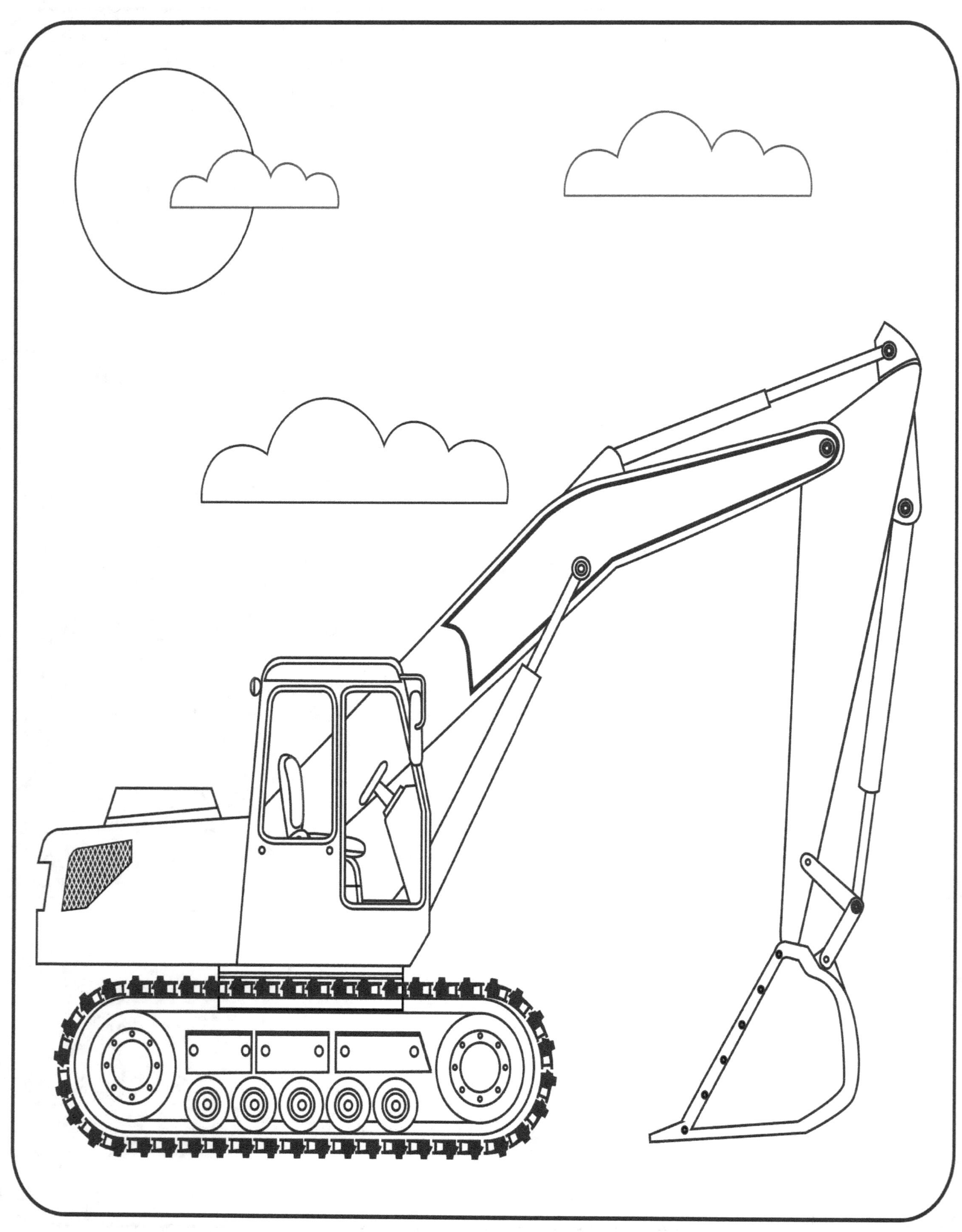

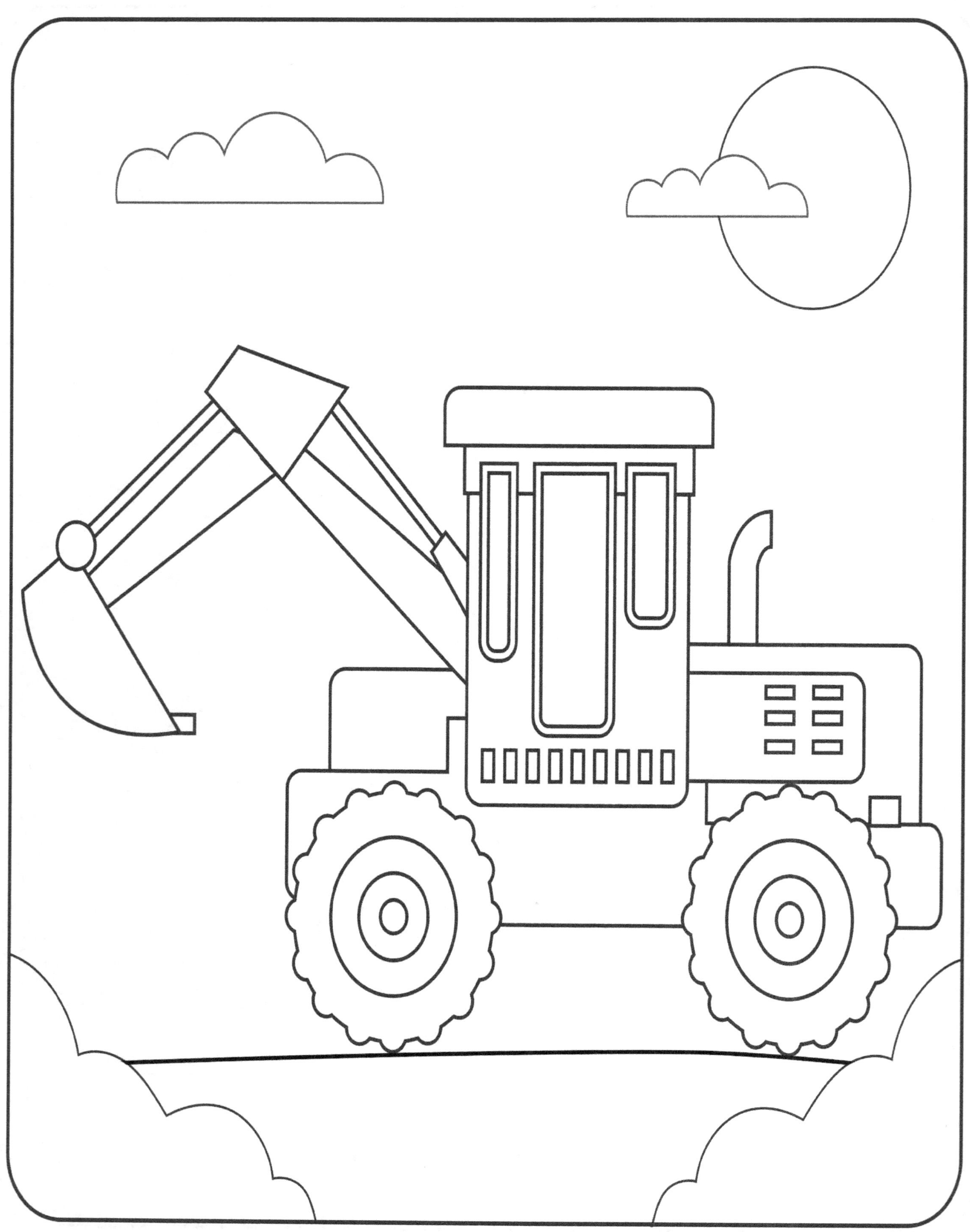

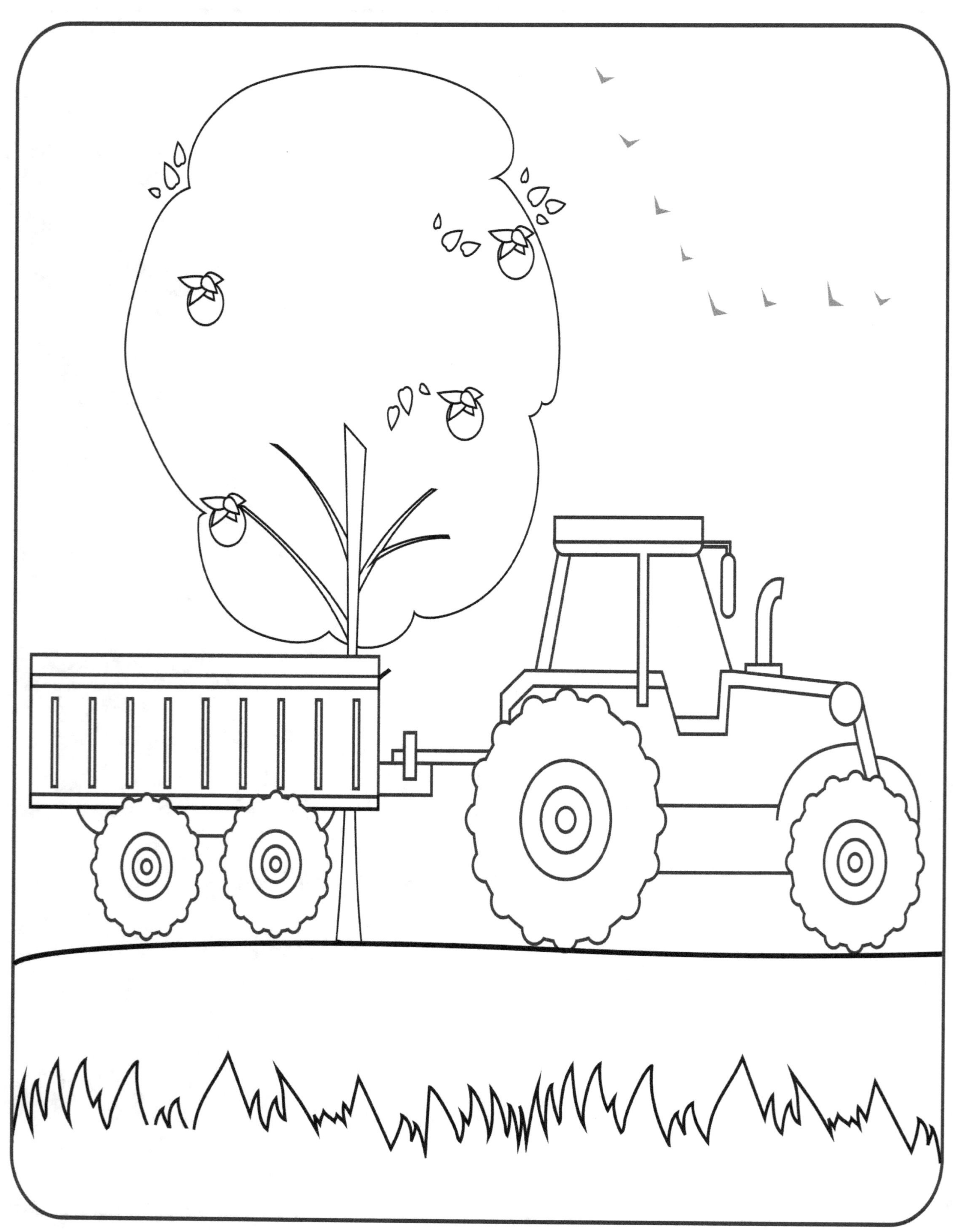

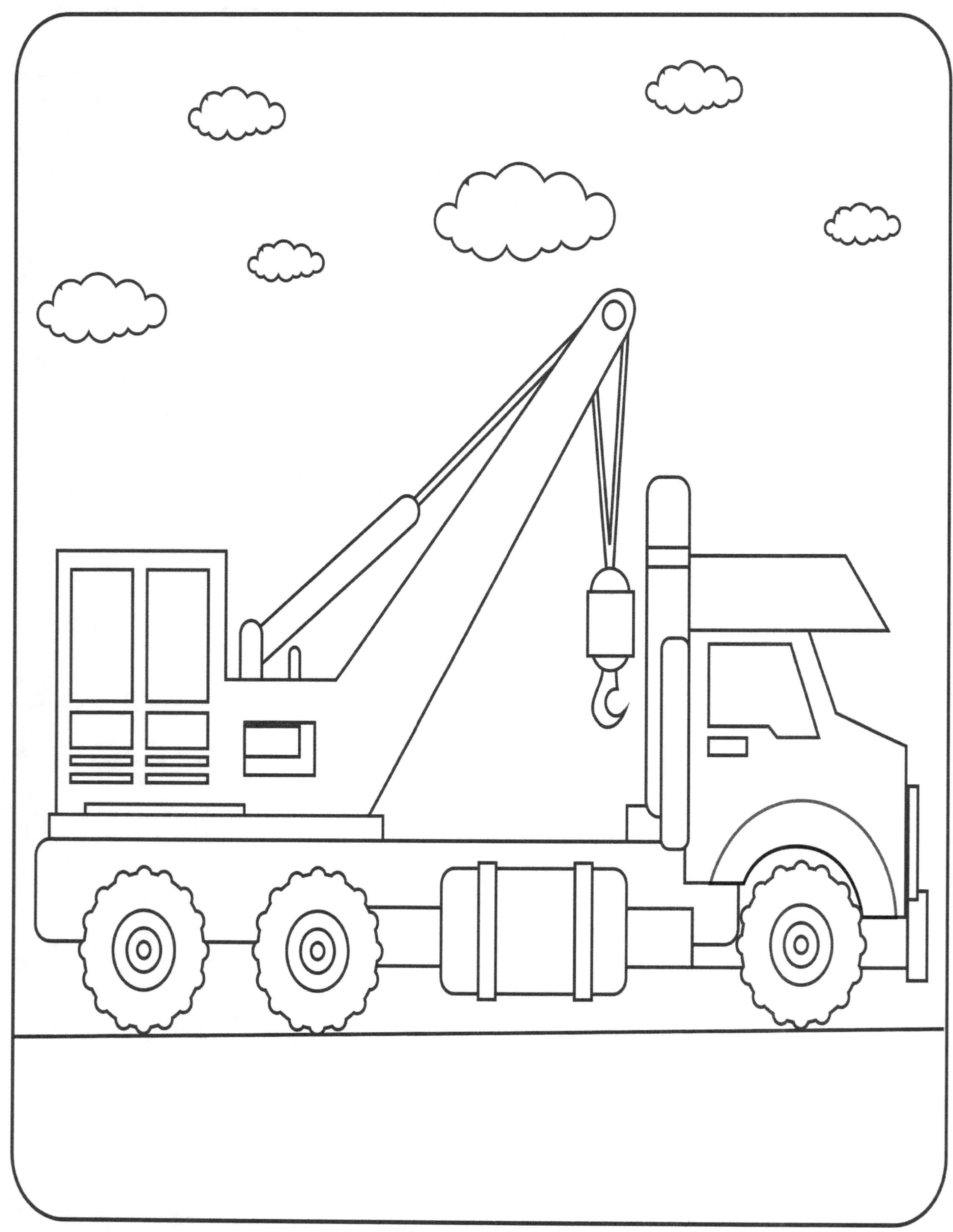

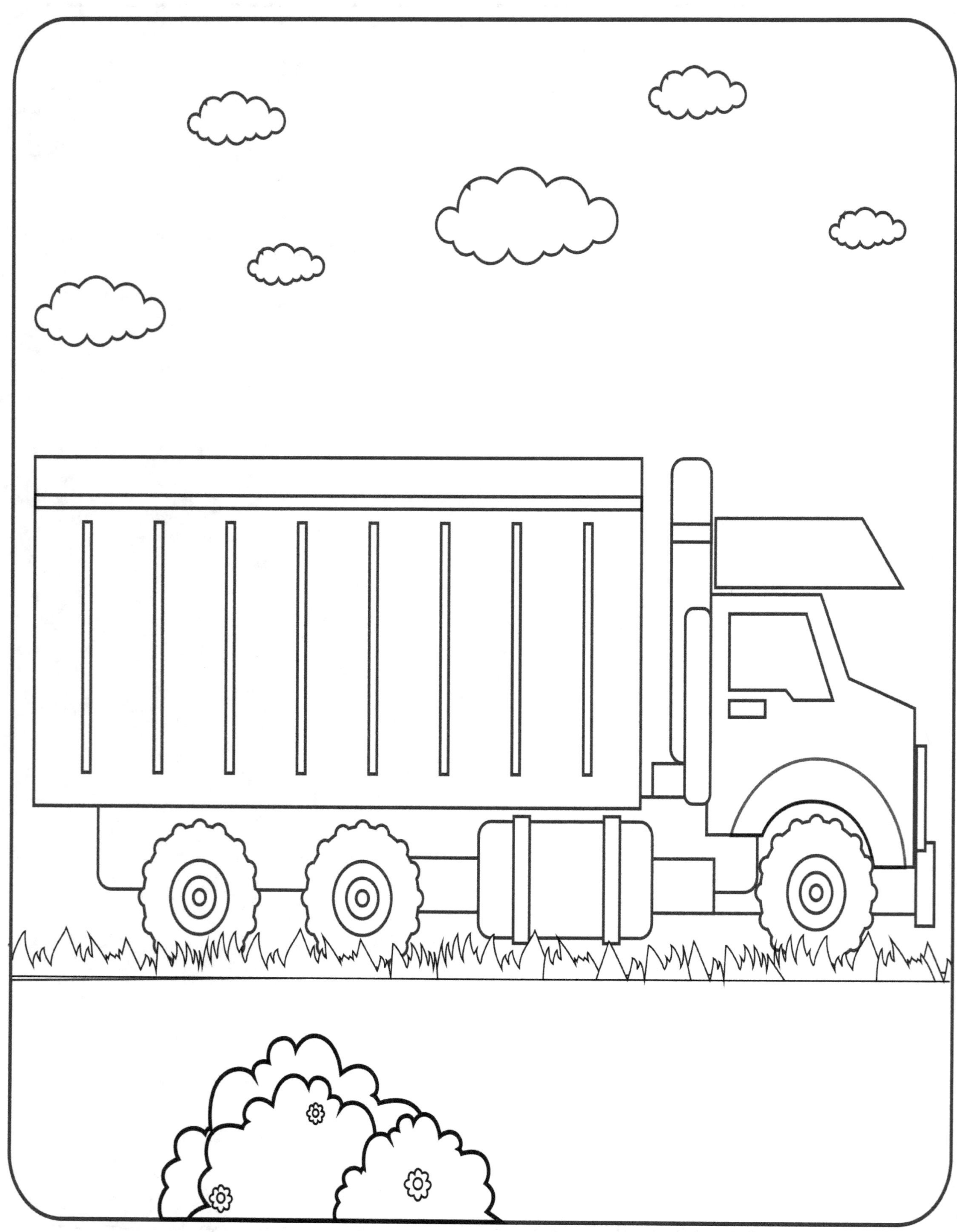

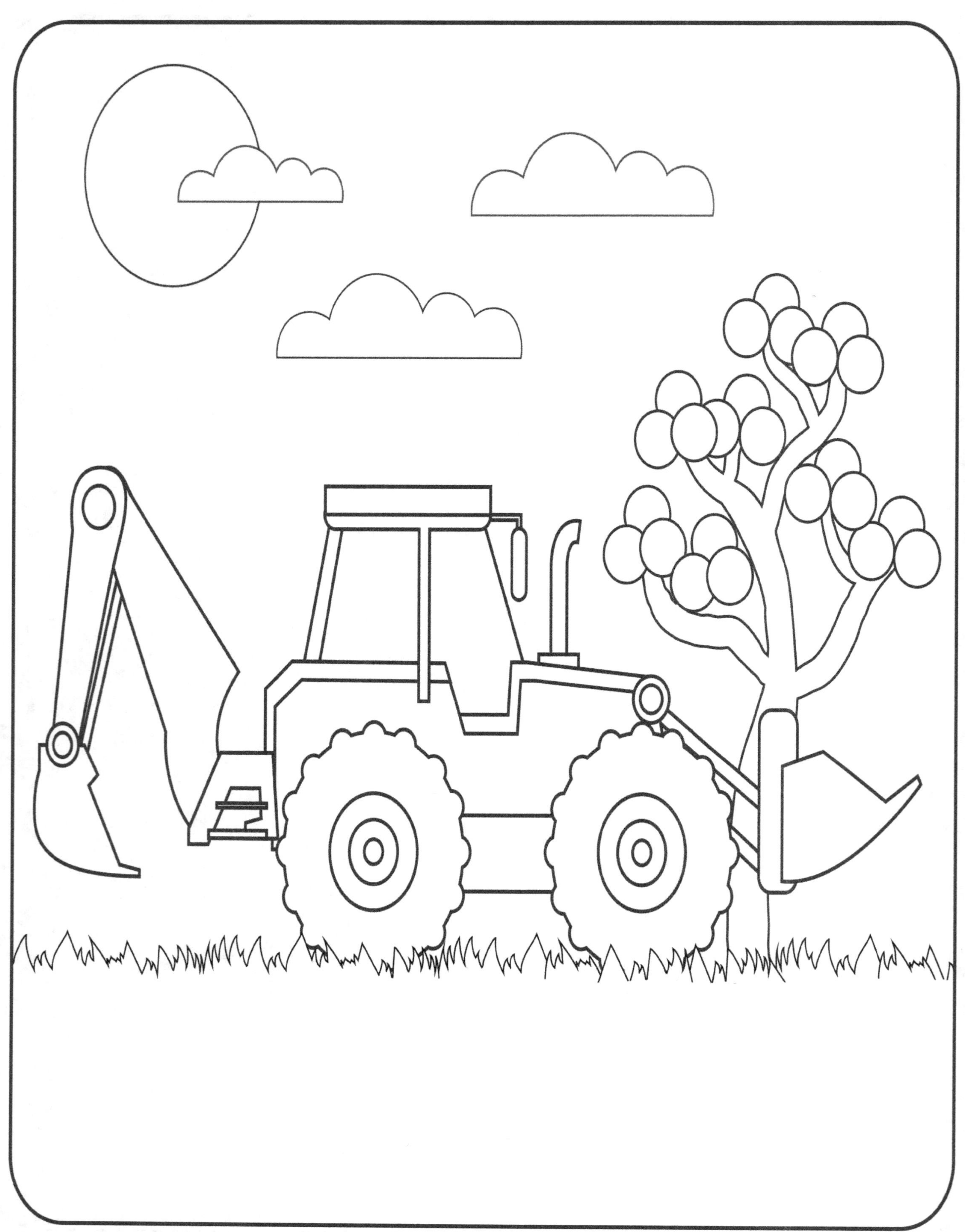

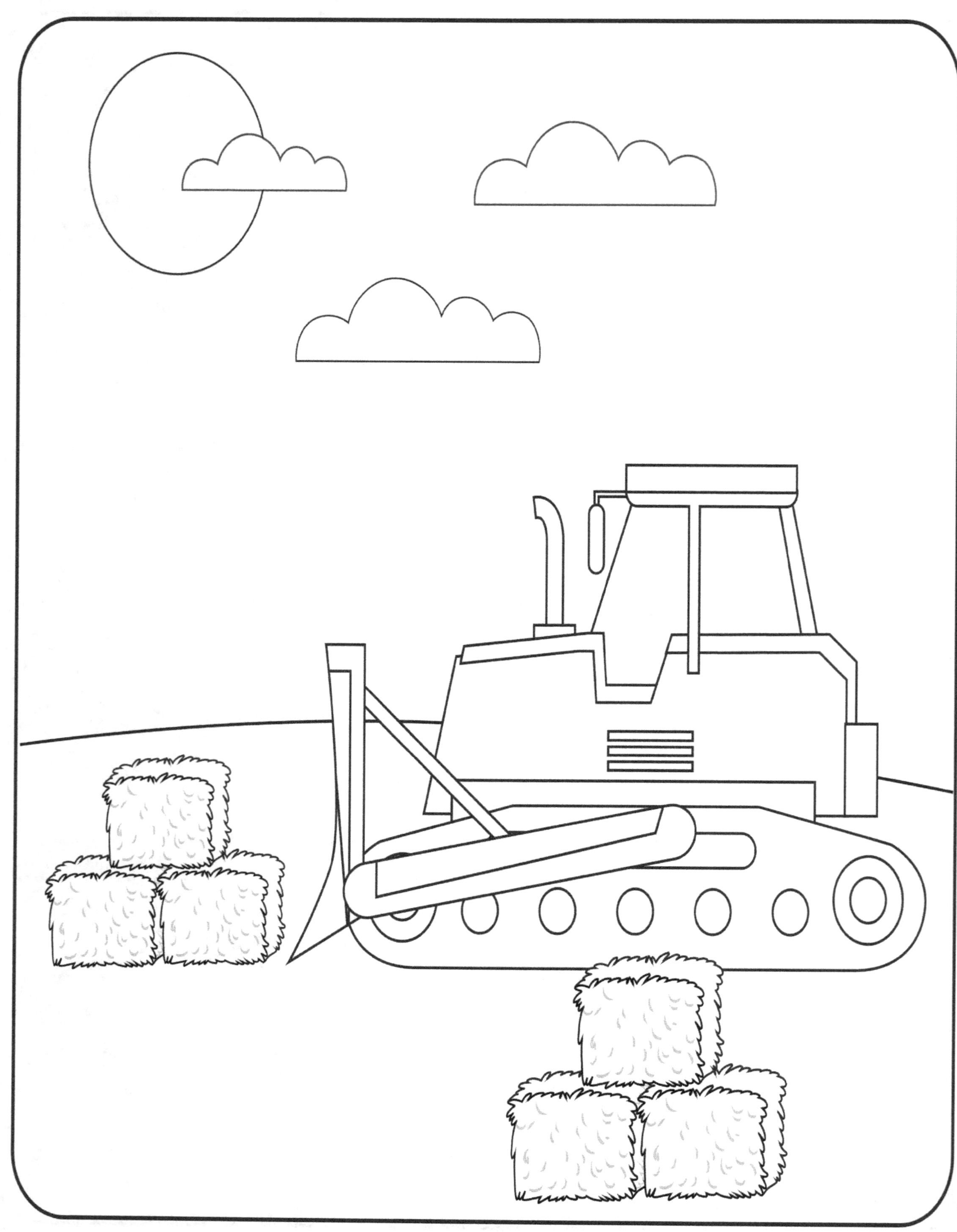

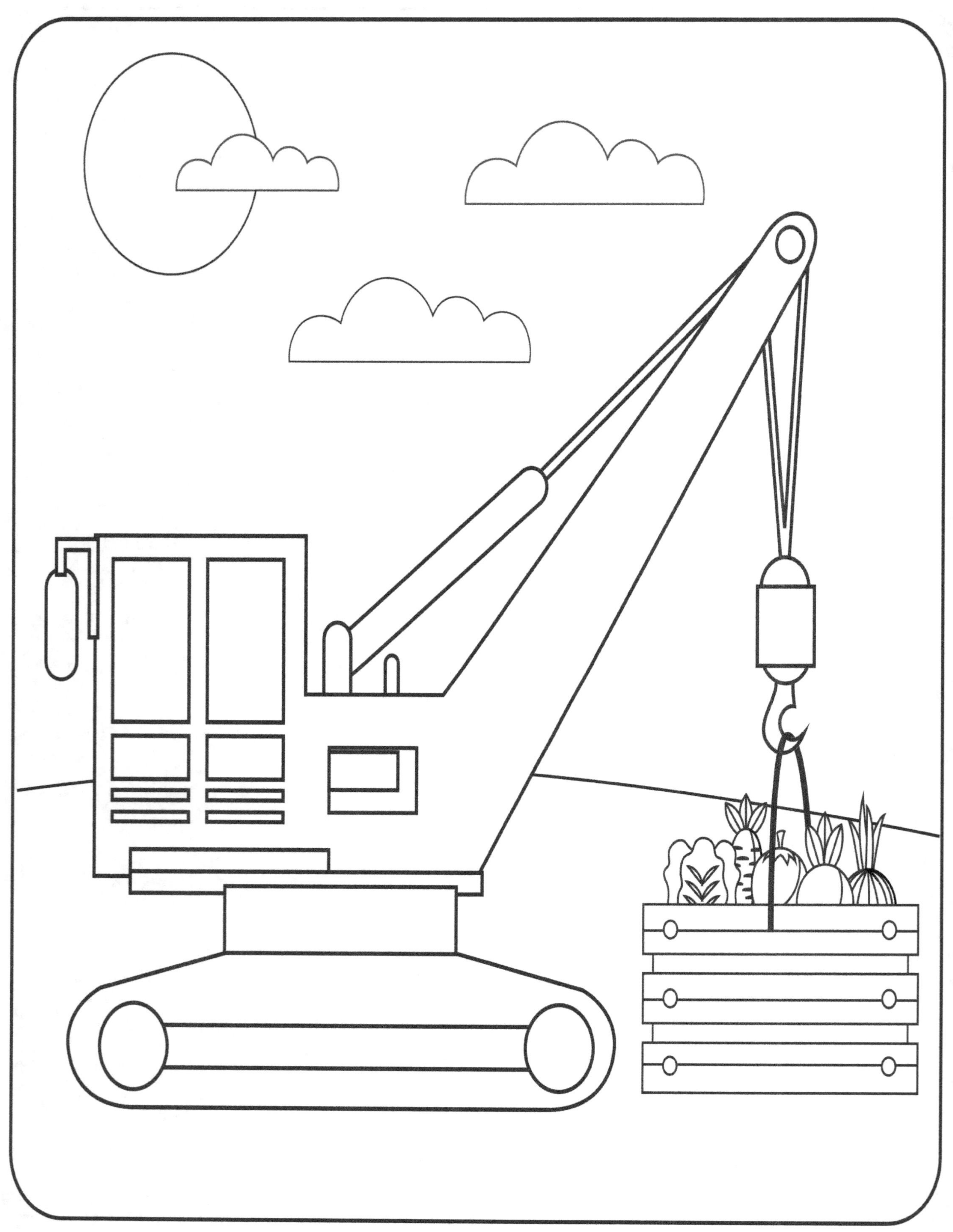

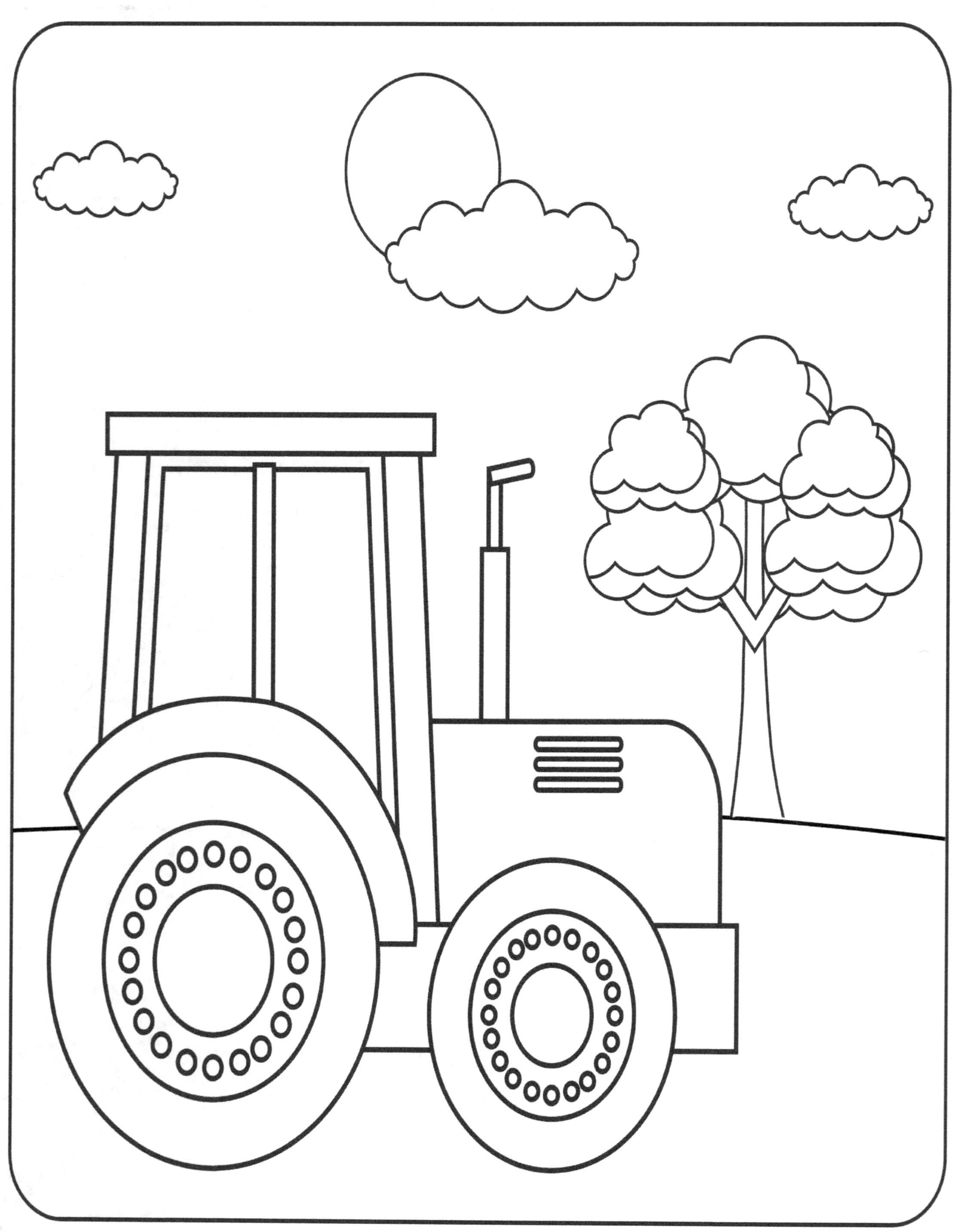

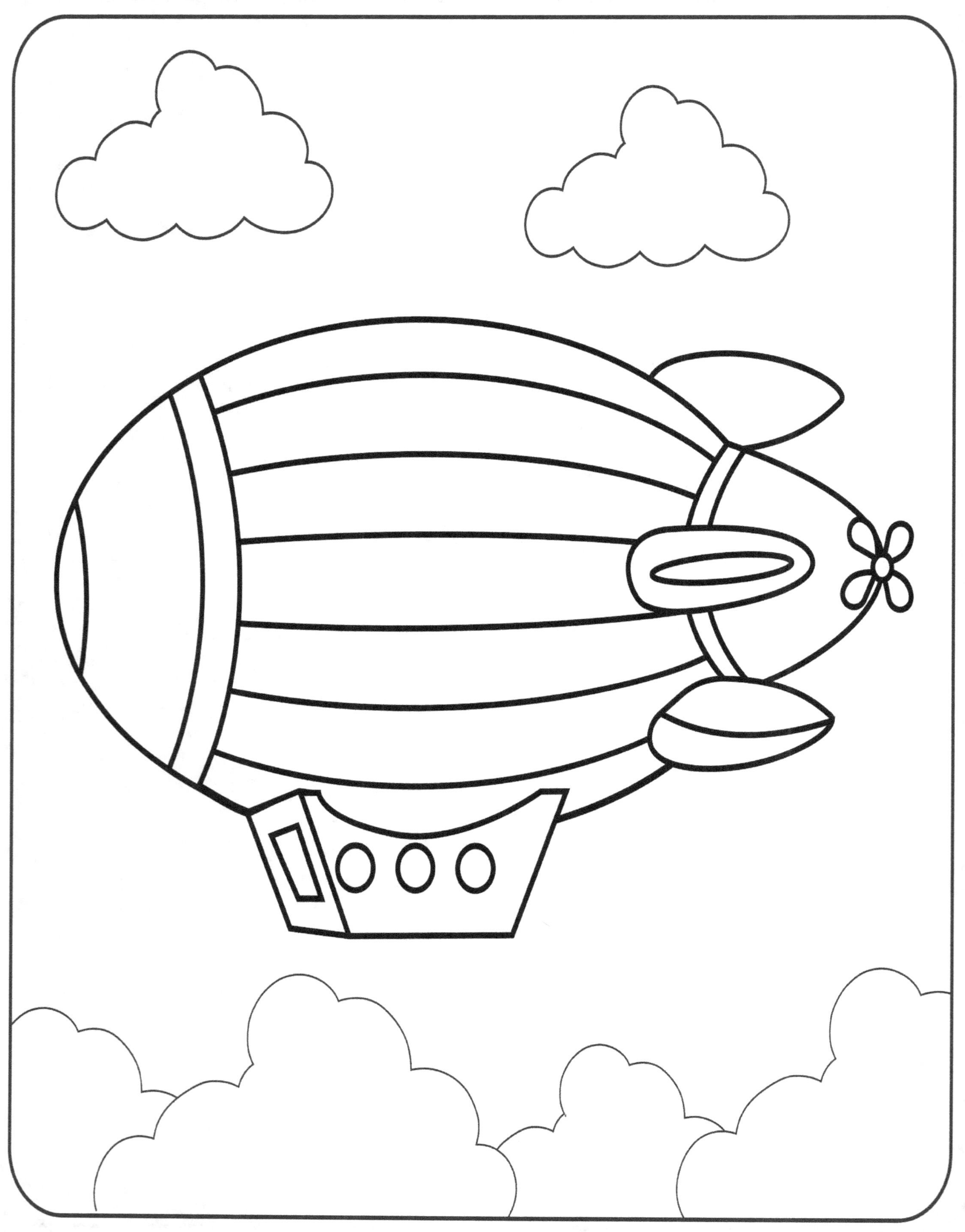

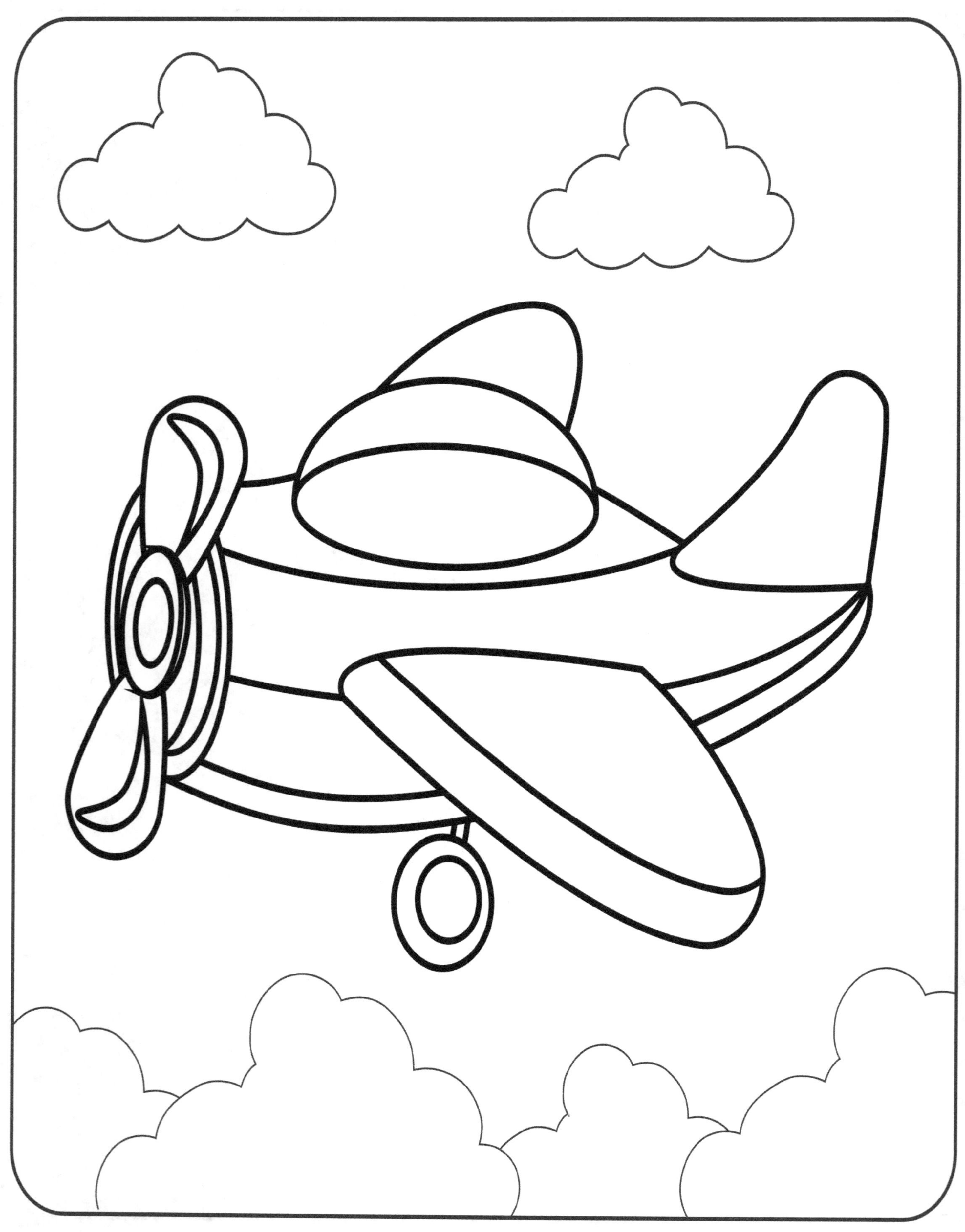

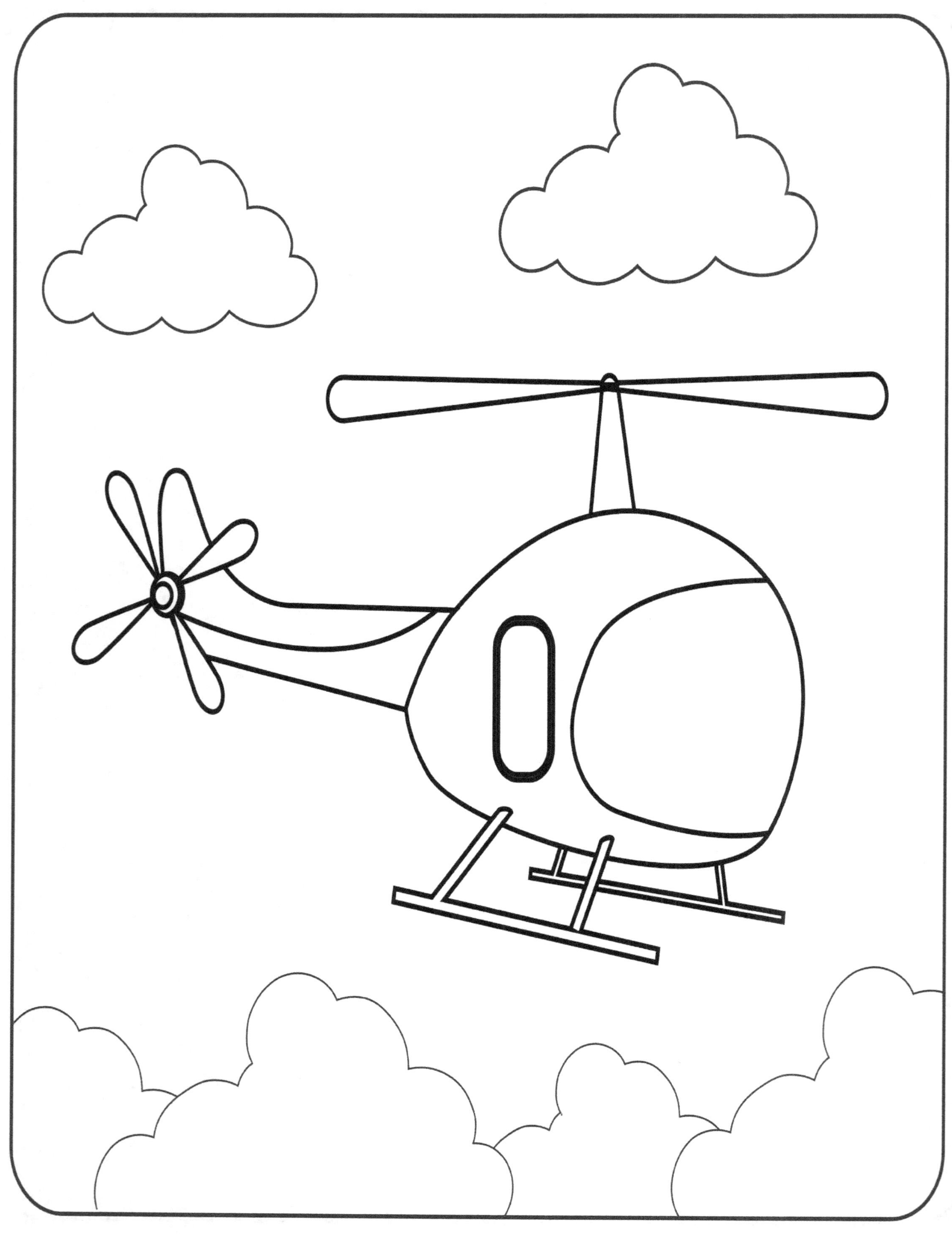

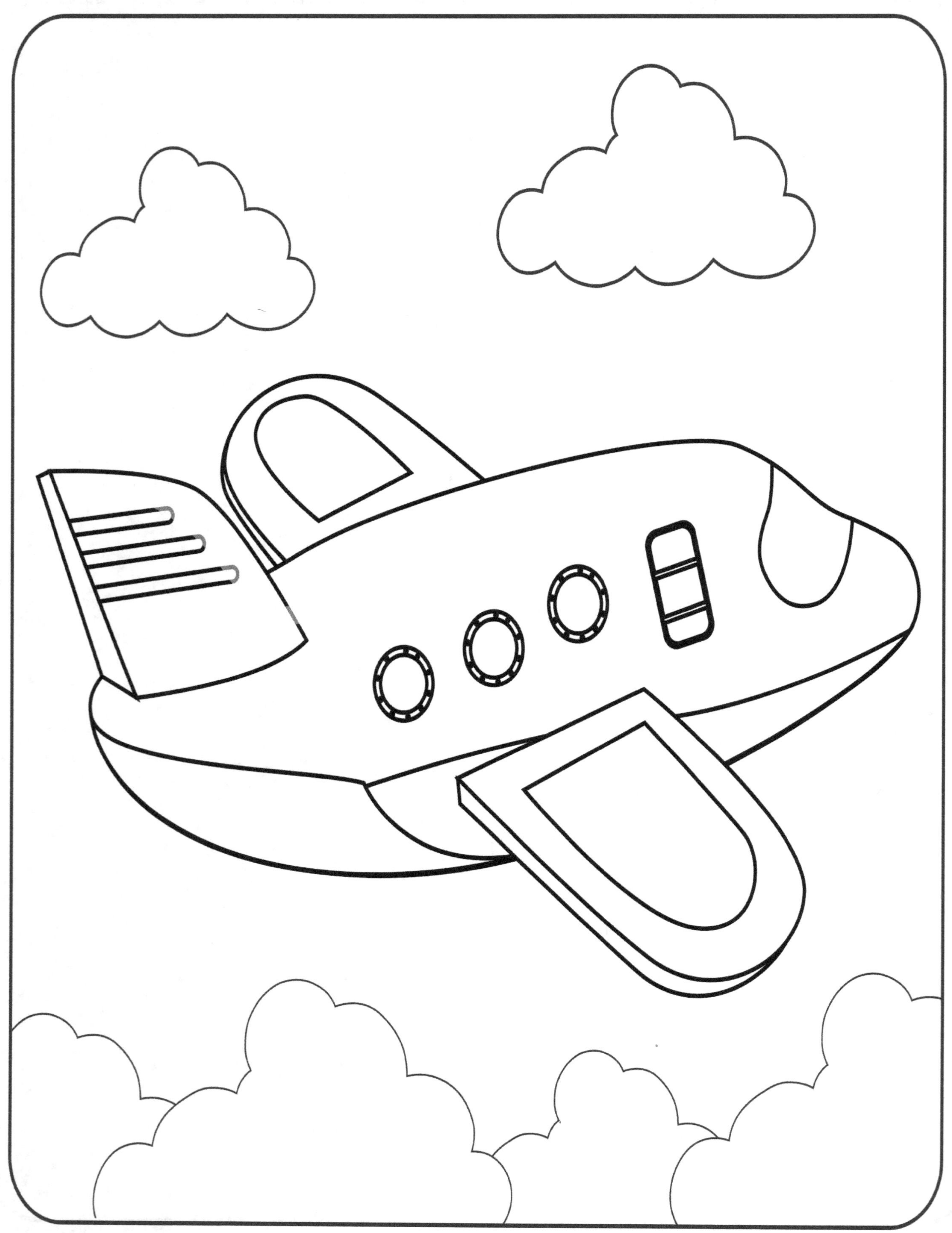

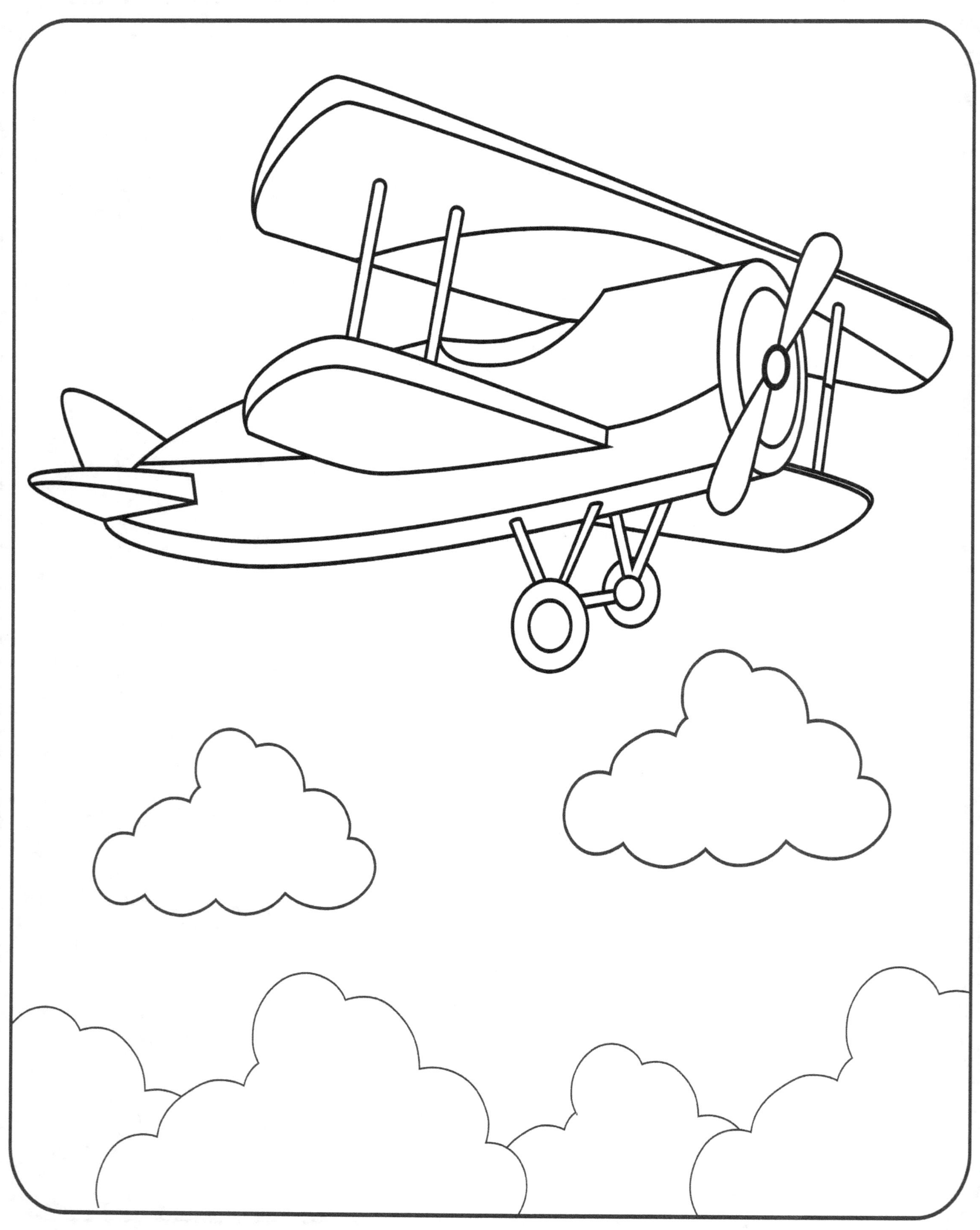

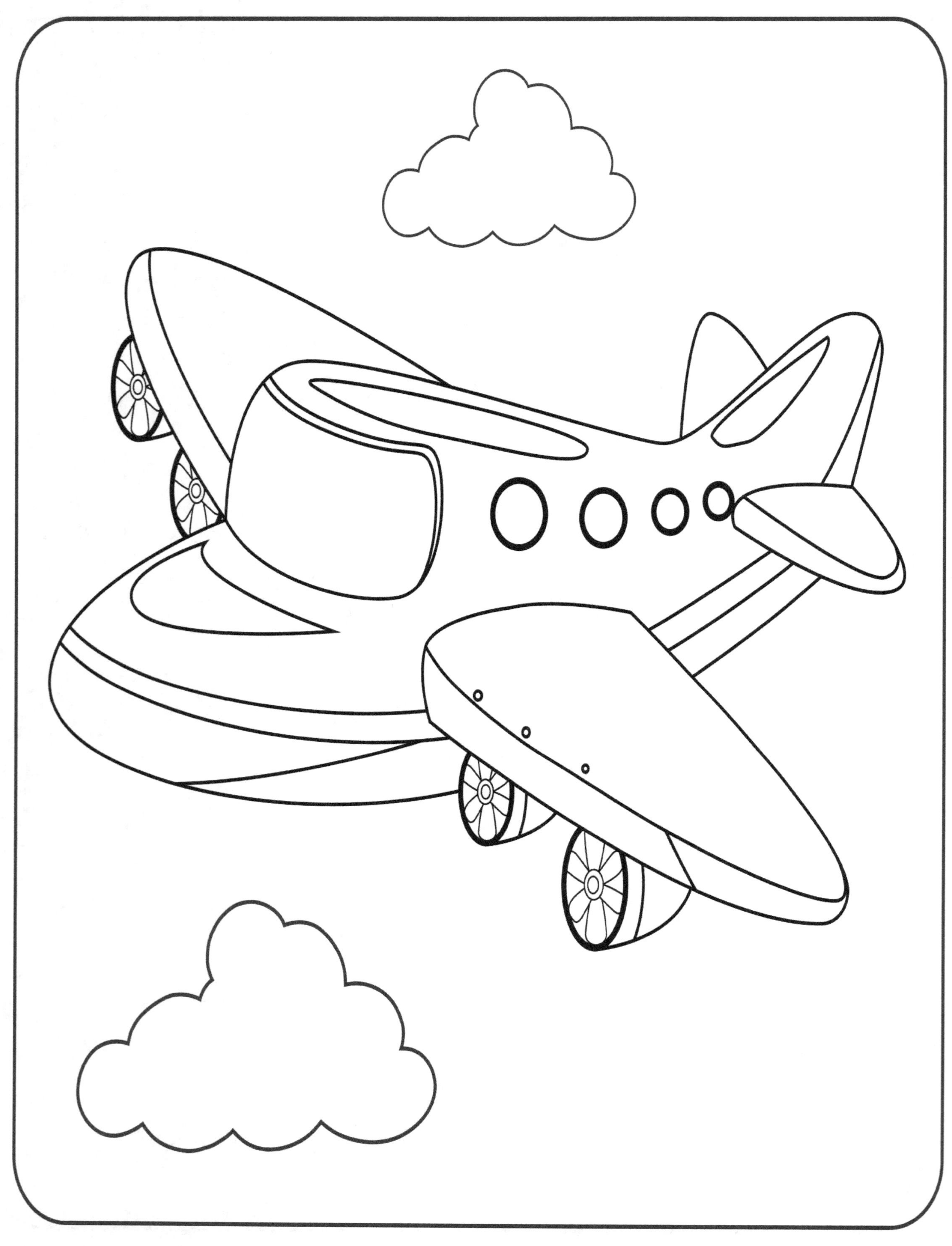

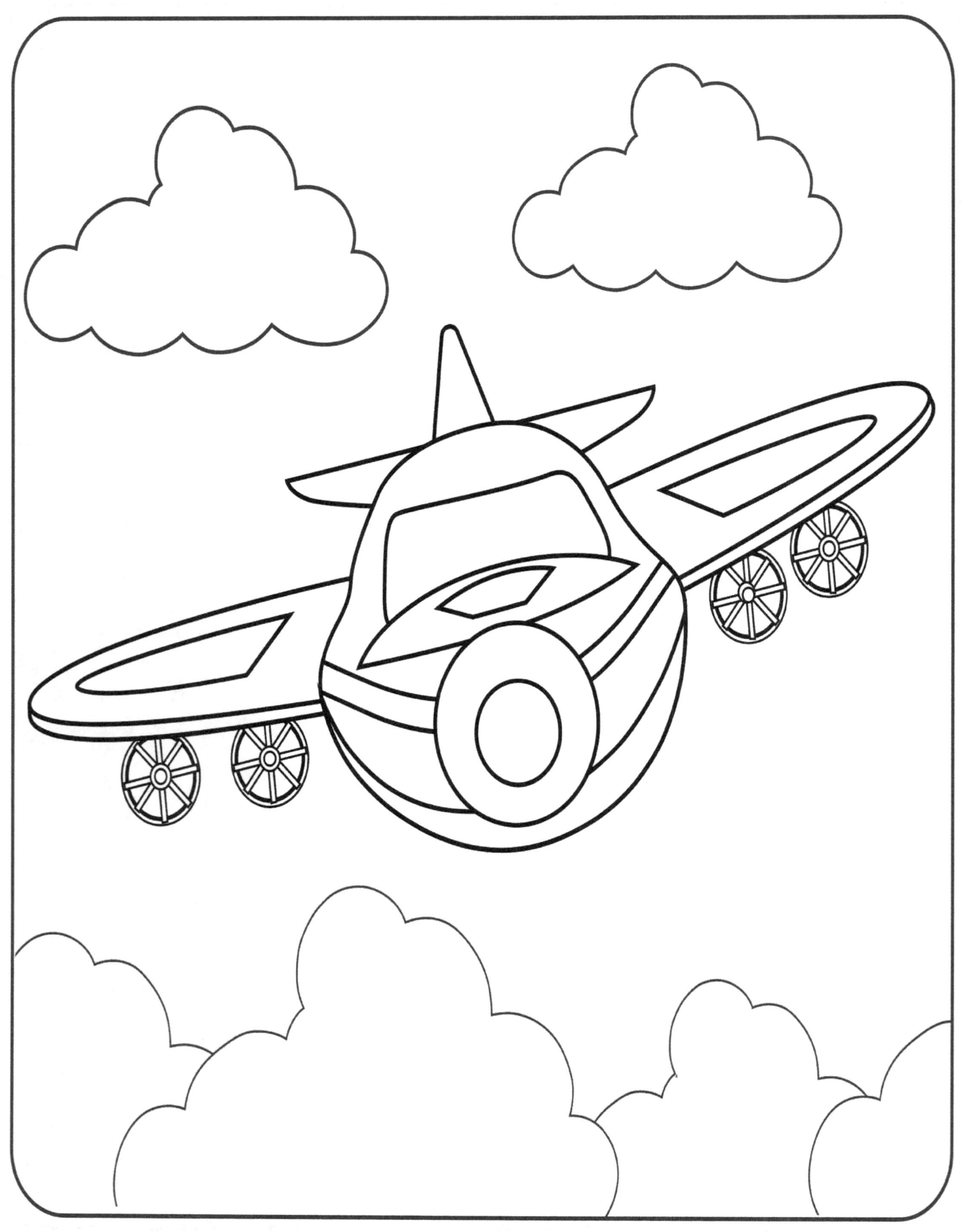

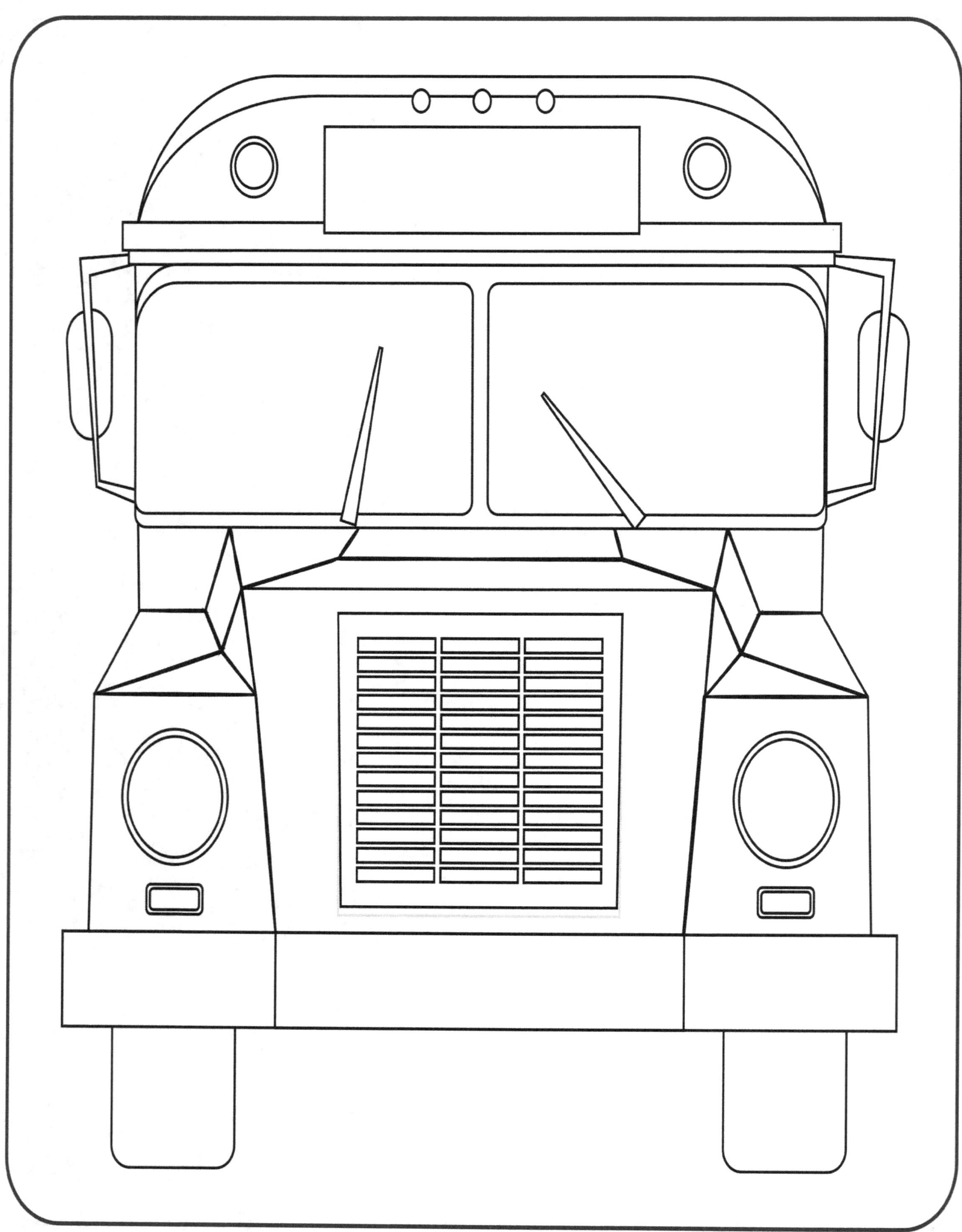

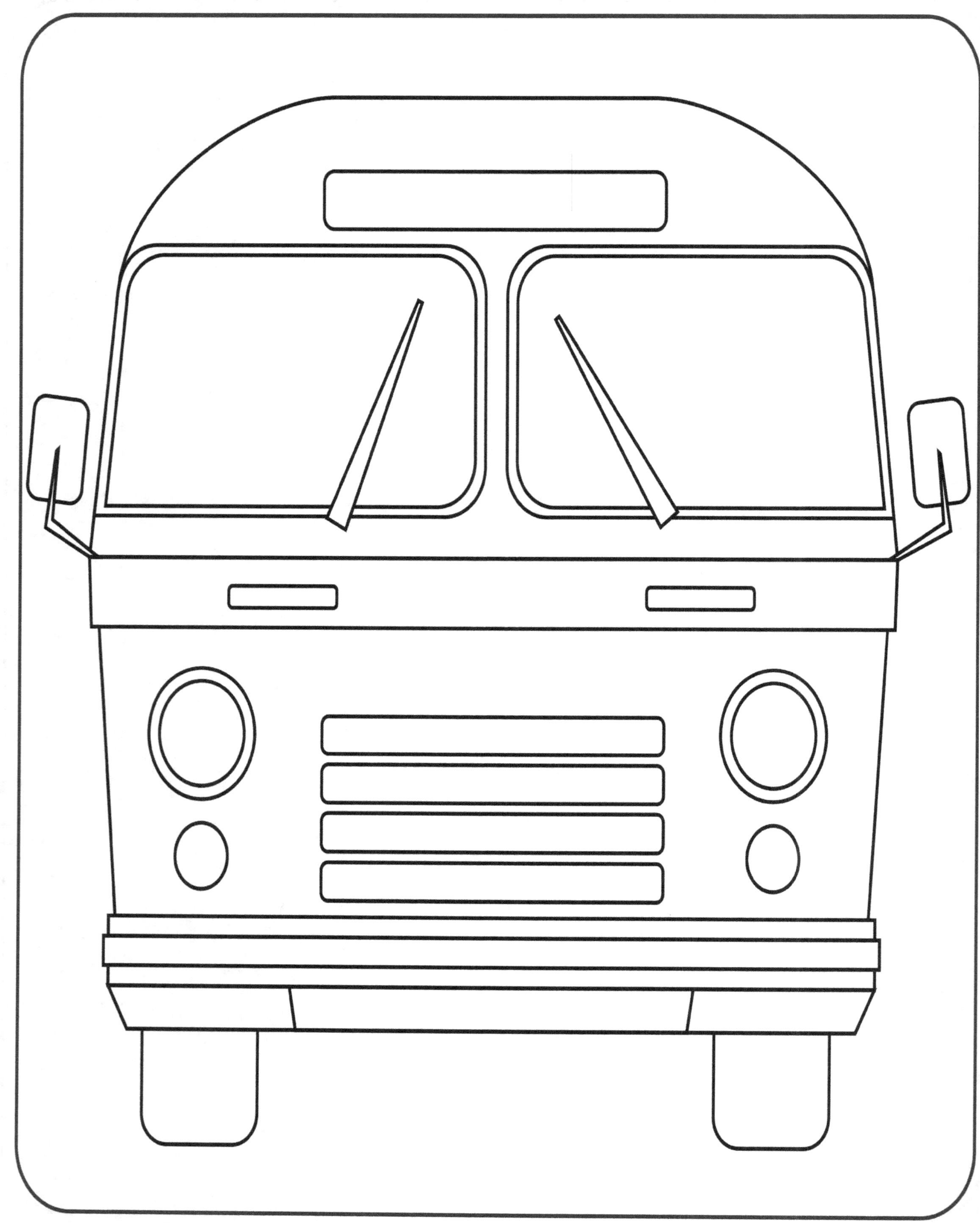

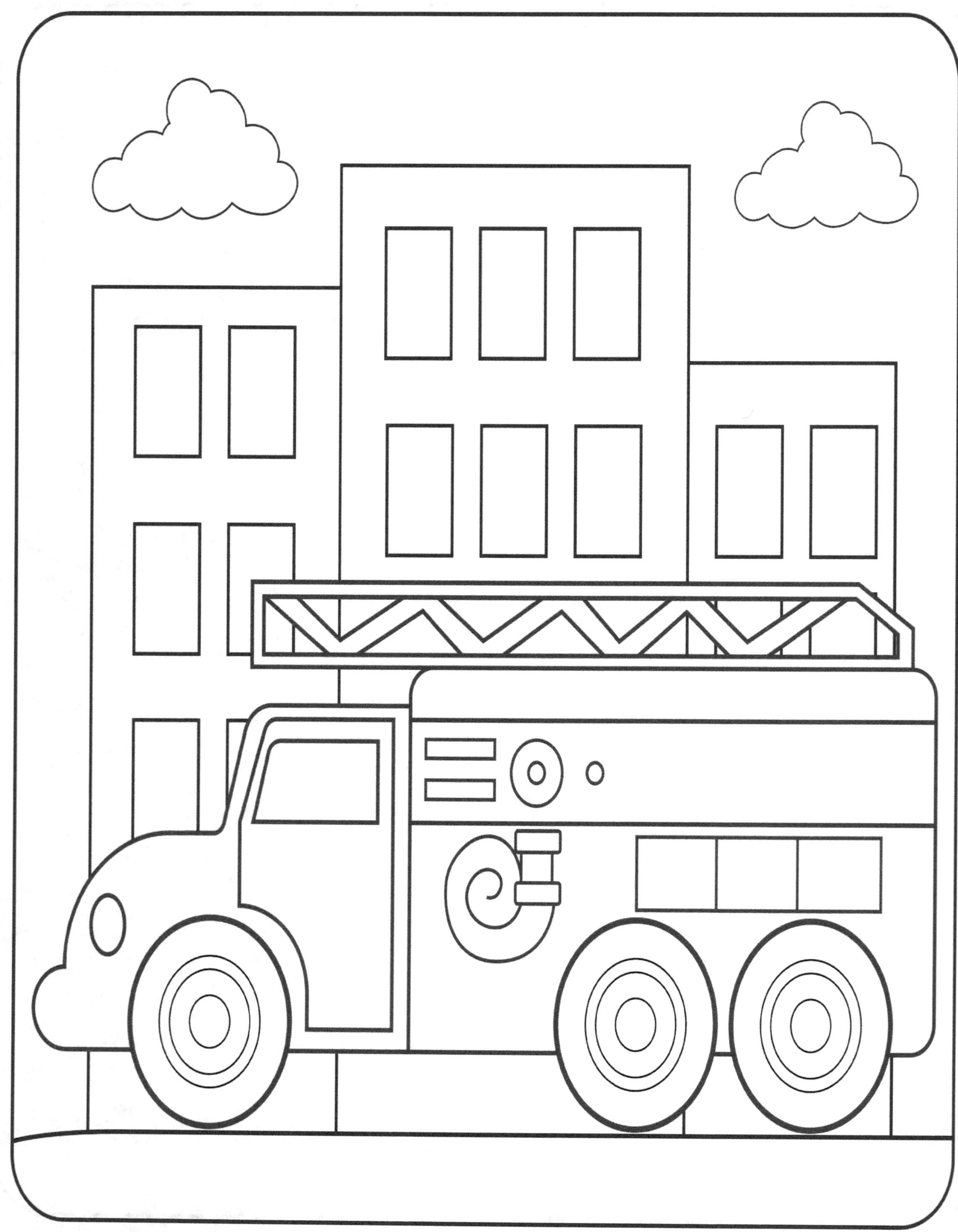

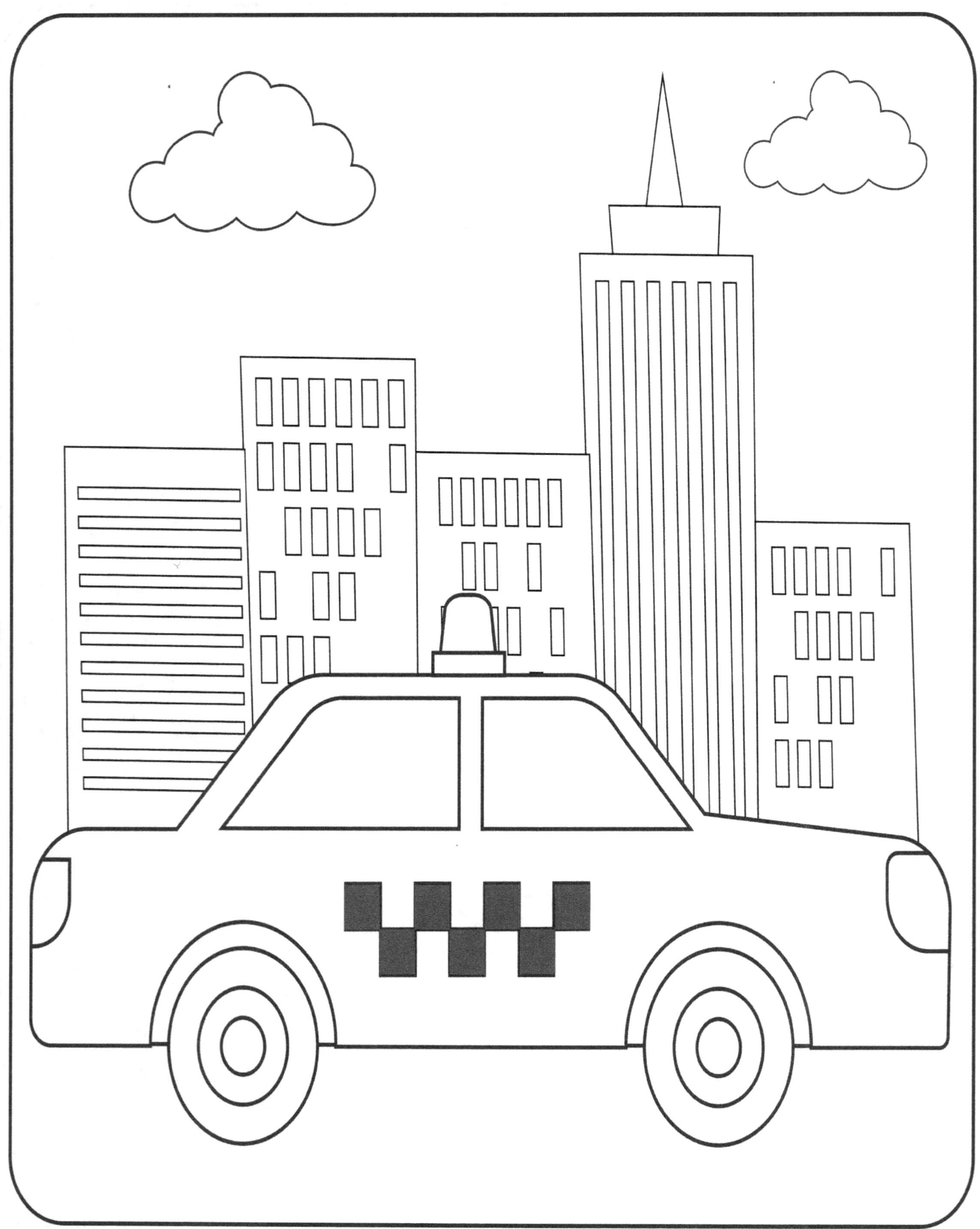

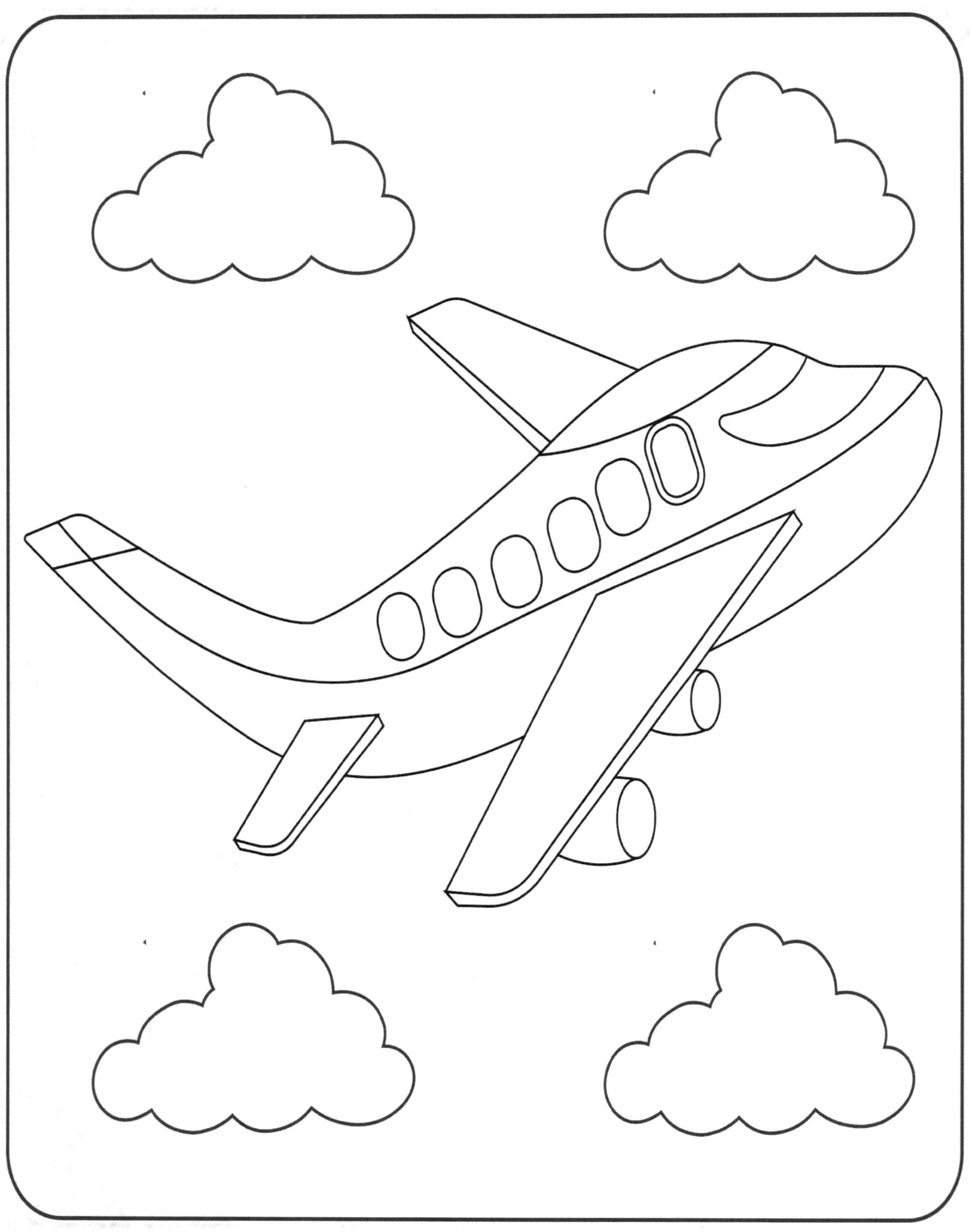